The Anger HABIT in RELATIONSHIPS

A Communication Handbook for Relationships, Marriages and Partnerships

Carl Semmelroth, PhD

SOURCEBOOKS, INC.®
NAPERVILLE, ILLINOIS

Copyright © 2005 by Carl Semmelroth, PhD
Cover and internal design © 2005 by Sourcebooks, Inc.
Sourcebooks and the colophon are registered trademarks of Sourcebooks, Inc.

All rights reserved. No part of this book may be reproduced in any form or by
any electronic or mechanical means including information storage and retrieval
systems—except in the case of brief quotations embodied in critical articles or
reviews—without permission in writing from its publisher, Sourcebooks, Inc.

This publication is designed to provide accurate and authoritative information
in regard to the subject matter covered. It is sold with the understanding that
the publisher is not engaged in rendering legal, accounting, or other professional service. If legal advice or other expert assistance is required, the services
of a competent professional person should be sought.—*From a Declaration of
Principles Jointly Adopted by a Committee of the American Bar Association and a
Committee of Publishers and Associations*

All brand names and product names used in this book are trademarks, registered
trademarks, or trade names of their respective holders. Sourcebooks, Inc., is not
associated with any product or vendor in this book.

This book is not intended as a substitute for medical advice from a qualified
physician. The intent of this book is to provide accurate general information in
regard to the subject matter covered. If medical advice or other expert help is
needed, the services of an appropriate medical professional should be sought.

Published by Sourcebooks, Inc.
P.O. Box 4410, Naperville, Illinois 60567-4410
(630) 961-3900
FAX: (630) 961-2168
www.sourcebooks.com

Library of Congress Cataloging-in-Publication Data

Semmelroth, Carl.
 The anger habit in relationships / by Carl Semmelroth.
  p. cm.
 ISBN 1-4022-0357-8 (alk. paper)
 1. Anger. 2. Man-woman relationships. 3. Habit breaking. I. Title.

BF575.A5S457 2005
152.4'7—dc22
                                        2004016837

Printed and bound in the United States of America
VP 10 9 8 7 6 5 4 3 2

The Anger HABIT in RELATIONSHIPS

To Will Crichton (1928–2002)
Philosopher, Poet, Teacher, and Friend

Table of Contents

Acknowledgments

Sara, my wife, has been my co-explorer of the means for building a satisfying marriage for forty-five years. To the extent that we have been able to achieve a calm and happy relationship, the credit is mainly Sara's. To the extent that this book reflects what it takes to do so, much credit is also hers.

My editor, Louise Waller, continues her patient molding and patting here and there with my writings. Magically, she transforms roughness into smoothness, incomprehensibility into straightforward prose. "You will not be there to explain what it means," will always ring in my mind while writing.

Professor Donald E. P. Smith, PhD, and Professor Dale M. Brethower both read the complete manuscript and made helpful suggestions. From the beginning they have cheered the ongoing project to help people with their anger.

Finally, the dedication of this book to the Canadian philosopher Will Crichton is a small token of the large influence he has had on my thinking and my life going back to Ann Arbor days in the late 1950s. His philosophical system, presented in *Foundations for a New Civilization* is rich with implications for the foundations and fabric of psychology. His view of feelings as being sensations of our tendencies to behave in certain ways is the view taken of anger in this book as well as elsewhere in my writings. Will's death was a painful loss to me, as well as to my family. We miss him.

Introduction
How to Use This Book

You need not have an awful relationship in order to benefit from at least some of the chapters in this book. It is intended for all partnerships.

The book's design makes it possible to use chapters independently. All readers do need to start with chapter 1. Then skip to those topics that concern your particular situation. If you are a therapist or workshop leader, you can easily design your own curriculum using chapters that fit the particular needs of your clients.

Making significant changes in relationships is even more difficult than changing individual behaviors. Our relationships are the parts of us that are the least in our control. Therefore, changing them requires commitments to doing things differently for a while before the changes we have made bear the fruits of satisfaction, increased calmness, and increased communication. Yes, it takes two to tango. But partners will never tango if each person waits for their partner to learn first.

Many exercises are supplied to help you apply what is being learned about relationships in general to your particular relationships. We strongly suggest that you keep a private notebook handy while working through the exercises. The more you actively respond and apply the material, the more likely you are to make lasting changes.

Chapter 1
Anger Is about Control

Alice and John, unhappily married for many years, are veterans of marriage counseling and weekend relationship workshops. On a beautiful Saturday morning, John gets up thinking how great it would be to play golf. Alice interrupts his thoughts with the comment, "It's going to be a beautiful day." John wonders what Alice has in mind for him to do. Maybe clean the gutters? His mood turns to irritation.

This seemingly innocent beginning to a summer weekend is the prelude to yet another weekend of anger and bitter feelings. Breakfast will not be complete before a sullen John will criticize Alice, and then a hurt Alice will become silent. After many years of honest effort to improve their relationship, Alice and John feel even more isolated from each other than before. Anger, bitterness, and hurt are their frequent companions. But they both remember how it was in the beginning of their marriage, and they bravely maintain a painful search to regain their lost intimacy.

> Neither Alice nor John realizes the destructive role that anger plays in their relationship. Neither recognizes the extent to which they depend on anger in their lives. They have been "taught" that it is healthy to express anger. They assume that other people must be good at "working through" their angry differences, even though they have never been able to do so. No one has explained to them what anger really is, how it works, and how destructive it is.
>
> Unfortunately, they will not find peace and happiness with each other while maintaining their anger. At this point they have no notion that they are each responsible for the anger and bitterness they experience. They continue to assume, like most people, that their spouses "make" them angry.

Anger in marriages and relationships is all too common. We all know the odds of staying married are about the same as winning a coin flip. Statistically, a happy, satisfying relationship is even less of a possibility. We can no longer afford the fiction that the biggest anger problem is that people don't express anger in a healthy way. The biggest anger problem is that there is too much of it and it is expressed all the time.

But haven't people always been angry? Three generations ago, when most people stayed married, anger was probably as pervasive as it is now. What is the difference between then and now that results in relationships ending while they mostly survived in our grandparents' time? The answer is that three generations ago anger made little difference in relationships because men were expected to control relationships anyway.

In order to understand this change, we need to understand what anger is and why we get angry. The feeling of anger is your awareness of your body preparing to physically attack someone. When we feel angry often, it means that we automatically, through habit, choose threatening others as a way to solve our problems. It means that we tend to solve all our problems by getting control over others.

Anger is preparation to control by threatening to attack others.

Verbal threats and angry facial expressions often cause others to change their behaviors. Others act to avoid our angry expressions. Because they produce immediate changes in the behaviors of others, our angry expressions are rewarded and easily become habitual. Using control gained through anger can become a favorite method to solve problems.

It is important to realize that seeking more control by becoming angry is a method we use to solve problems. When it becomes our favorite method for dealing with most problems, we have the Anger Habit or the Control Habit. When we use anger to solve most problems we experience in a particular area of our lives, we have a Relationship Anger Habit or a Work Anger Habit or a Parenting Anger Habit. For example, an otherwise mild-mannered person may have

We need to understand what anger is and why we get angry.

only one way of dealing with relationship problems—seeking dominance in the relationship, or at least finding out who is dominant. Then the dominant person gets to call the shots. This is the wolf-pack solution to all relationship problems. The "top dog" threatens, and the others fall in line.

Anger is about solving problems of a certain kind by gaining control.

Now we can see why marriages and relationships in general are in such trouble today. The serious introduction of an expectation of equality in relationships has changed anger from a useful tool for male-dominated or male-role-dominated relationships into a poison for equality-based relationships. Yes, both men and women used to try for control in relationships. Women used threats—such as withdrawal of affection, hurt feelings, and inattention to servile tasks—in a struggle for control with their husbands. However, men held the trump cards: economic and legal status that allowed men total control over the welfare of other members of the family. As undesirable as male domination was, it preserved the marriage, just as alpha individuals (established dominant individuals) preserve a group of wolves or chimpanzees. Unlike marriages, wolf packs stay together. Men used to hold the biggest stick in battles for control, therefore anger didn't end relationships.

What could women who were in angry adversarial relationships do? They had fewer options for avoiding their husbands' anger-enforced control than their children had. Their major coping mechanisms were covert counterattack techniques, such as displays of unhappiness and hurt feelings or living in submissive "love my master who takes care of me" relationships.

Women today, by and large, expect to be equal partners in relationships. Equality in relationships is incompatible with control by either member. Because anger is about control, not equality, relationships cannot easily survive anger.

Equality in loving relationships requires voluntary association.

We are in the middle of an important revolution. Just as humankind has struggled to build political institutions that free individuals, today's couples are struggling to build the cultural institutions of marriage and couple relationships on a foundation of freedom. As we substitute voluntary association for controlled association, we struggle to leave behind the ugly trappings of control that made marriage work when it was a male-controlled institution. The simple fact is that loving and intimate relationships between equals must be voluntary.

Anger means attempts to control, and this erases equality. One person in control requires that another must forgo control of his or her own behavior. Equality is driven out. Freedom is driven out. And those things that can only be given freely—love and intimacy—are driven out.

It isn't a matter of learning to express anger "appropriately." There can be no appropriate use of attempted control among equals, except when it is justified by a broken promise or agreement. And when broken promises and agreements occur in relationships, it is the breaking of those agreements, not anger, that troubles the relationship. When one person is unfaithful in a relationship that has agreed on monogamy, anger is an attempt to enforce the broken contract. It would be perverse to think of the partner's angry response as inappropriate, assuming it falls somewhat short of homicide. But is anger necessary and natural?

The need to express anger lies in the idea that unexpressed anger will build up and explode. Confronting and communicating are often recommended as ways to avoid this problem. If you were a hydraulic machine, and anger was a hydraulic liquid that built up pressure when it had no place to go, then, yes, you would need to find some way to "let off" the pressure. But anger is not like pressure in a steam engine or hydraulic liquid in a hose. Anger is a set of behaviors. And unfortunately, many of those behaviors are habits.

Ask yourself: Do other sets of behavior—such as being pleasant to people or acting in a loving way toward people or laughing with others—build up like steam when you don't perform them for a while? Aren't you even less likely to be pleasant to others if you haven't been pleasant for a while? Doesn't it really work the other way around? That is, if you express love often or joy often or laugh a lot, aren't you even more likely to keep on doing so in the future? Anger works that way too. The more you do it, the more likely you are to do it.

Expressing anger doesn't decrease anger; quite the contrary, it increases it.

Sometimes people smother their anger. This amounts to acting and feeling like someone who is subordinate to and less important than others. Often, people who smother anger are treated so badly that they break out of the submissive stance and "let someone have it." In the short run, this can be good for a relationship. It sets the other person back on their heels and for a time there is an understanding that "you don't tread on me." However, in the long run, these explosions, or "expressions," perpetuate the feeling that the relationship is basically adversarial and one has to have good fighting skills to maintain it. This adversarial attitude will eventually drive out any feeling of voluntary living and loving together.

Feeling angry means that you, through habit, have chosen attack and control as your problem-solving tool. Having a problem with your anger means that you use attack and control to solve many problems in your life. Choosing other ways to solve problems does not require smothering anger or expressing anger. It just means you no longer automatically reach for that one tool, attack, to solve your problems.

This book teaches alternative ways for solving problems that arise in relationships, ways that do not require attacking or preparing to attack your partner. If love and intimacy are going to be preserved in your relationships, then the relationship must feel free to both of you. Love and intimacy cannot be lassoed and tied up. Force kills them. Control kills them. Anger kills them.

This book guides you through the learning of new habits for the solution of problems that you commonly "solve" with anger. Learning alternatives to anger, other than smothering it or expressing it, reduces its presence in your relationships and helps preserve the sense of freedom and equality necessary for continued loving and caring.

Your reward for working to reduce anger in your relationships is much greater than just reducing "blowups" or even stopping the destructive and irrational behaviors that accompany anger. These are worthy, important, and satisfying goals of anger management.

But this book guides you toward much more than the management or control of your anger.

Anger reduces your sense of freedom. It makes communication difficult, if not impossible, and without communication, relationships wither on the vine. Anger impairs your intelligence. It leads your relationships into a perpetual desire to either control or to escape control. It takes you farther and farther from your desire, an intimate and loving connection with another human being.

The rewards for giving up the anger habit in your relationships are a calm mind, a sense of freedom, better communication with another person, release from the quest for power, and the comfort and vitality that come with a life that encourages each other, rather than a life bent on controlling each other.

Thirty years of counseling couples has taught me that civilization has not yet truly come to the family. Patterns of family interaction that individuals bring to marriage remain those based on adversarial living. The problems of adversaries are resolved only by power and control. Individuals enter their important relationships with the ideal of equality, but come to them equipped with weapons, armor, and the anger habit. Happy and lasting relationships require voluntary cooperation, freedom of association, respect for one another, and keeping of agreements; in other words, good relationships require civilized behavior in the home.

It is important for you to complete the exercises contained in each chapter in order to achieve these goals. Just understanding your anger habit will not change it. It takes practice to develop a new attitude—an attitude of problem solving in place of controlling and attacking. Examples of "answers" are included with every exercise as a guide for your own written responses. Sometimes it helps to get started by copying one of the examples and letting it become yours as you write.

It will also be helpful for you to find a friend, counselor, or family member with whom you can discuss issues that arise as you work through the lessons. If you are using the book in an anger management class or group, the group will supply the opportunity to discuss issues as they occur.

Finally, as you work through the chapters in this guidebook, you will find advice on how to keep a record of your successes at changing the way you deal with problems. Examples are provided, but you will need a diary or private notebook to keep a record of your progress. It is important to recognize and record your successes. They will help you sustain your efforts and serve as models for you to continue solving problems without resorting to the anger habit.

Chapter 2
Transaction and Interaction in Relationships

Sue's striking blue eyes glisten and then moisten as Tom's deep voice gets even deeper. She realizes that he's on his way to asking her to date exclusively for a while. She's thrilled, but a little surprised. Tom has made a big thing of his independence and has repeatedly cautioned her that he is not a "one-woman" man. He said he just wants to be friends and have someone to do things with. Sue doesn't hesitate to hug Tom and tell him she wants the same thing he does.

On a Wednesday, a month later, Sue sits at work but her mind is elsewhere. She hasn't heard from Tom since last Sunday. They usually talk every day. By this time in the week they usually have the weekend planned. Sue knows Tom doesn't like to be called at work, but she can't stand it anymore and dials his work number. Someone (female) answers, and after a long wait Tom picks up the phone.

"I'm sorry to call you at work, but I was worried."

Tom speaks evenly but with unmistakable irritation, "What do you mean worried? I'm okay. I've just been busy."

Sue sets her jaw and her voice goes cold and hard in a way that Tom has never heard before. "Sorry to bother you." She hangs up carefully.

That evening Tom is waiting at Sue's door when she gets home.

"What do you want?" she says. "I thought you were busy."

"Oh come on, Sue. I'm sorry if I did something wrong, but I don't see what the big deal is."

The voice that Tom heard earlier on the phone comes back. With ice crystals dripping from every word, Sue says, "It's okay, Tom. Don't worry about it. I'm the one who is at fault. I should have known what you're like. You told me, for cripe's sake. I was stupid enough to think I meant something to you. But as you said right at the beginning, you just want someone to do things with."

Sue and Tom battle for half the night but end up in each other's arms. This is the first of countless fights they will have over the next several years. What happened to their good relationship?

Tom and Sue, like many couples, start out with a small—but important—misunderstanding. And, as the saying goes, a small mistake in the beginning is a large one in the end.

Tom and Sue began their relationship by mixing up their agreements with their expectations. When they said they would "go together," they made an agreement. That agreement was exactly like a contract. Sue said she would not go out with other men in exchange for Tom's agreement not to go out with other women. They set up an exclusive dating arrangement.

In the course of spending time together, Tom and Sue got into a rhythm. They went out almost every Friday and Saturday night.

They ate at the same places on Saturday nights. They talked on the phone nearly every weeknight. Because they were doing so many things regularly, they came to expect that those things would continue to happen.

Tom and Sue interacted week after week in similar ways and so they expected these interactions to occur. But Tom and Sue did not have a specific agreement to call each other every day. We can divide their activities into two kinds. They did some things because they had an agreement to do them. They did some things that were simply interactions with each other. This is true for all human relationships.

Some activities are transactional. They must be carried out because we have made an agreement to carry them out. They are contractual, like Sue and Tom agreeing to go together. Some activities are simple interactions. They may be expected because they often occur, but they are not part of an agreement. They are not required, like Sue and Tom calling each other daily.

Tom and Sue started their relationship with very few transactions. The big one was to date exclusively. Others were temporary agreements like, "I'll call you on Tuesday." Once made, these kinds of "promises" are binding, like any other transaction.

If someone breaks an agreement, a contract, we have the right to either hold them to it or the right to end the agreement. So, if Sue had seen Tom out with another woman, she would have the natural right to call him on it in no uncertain terms. Or if she decided that he wasn't someone who could be trusted to keep agreements, she could call off the arrangement. Such is the nature of transactions.

Trouble arises when common interactions become expected and then get treated as if they were part of an agreement. What used to be done out of a freely expressed love and caring then becomes an obligation. When common interactions become transactions without ever talking about them, they are no longer felt to be voluntary and are apt to feel like obligations that are out of the person's control.

What happened to Sue and Tom is that their relationship started out feeling good to both of them. It had a few agreed-upon transactions, but most of what they did with each other was done freely. Most of their behaviors with each other were not, and did not feel like, obligations. As they accumulated time together, they accumulated expectations, like "He should call because he hasn't called today" or "She should agree to go out Friday night because we always do." These expectations were turned into obligations.

Sue and Tom, like the rest of us, have the right to confront each other when one doesn't live up to an obligation. As they converted more and more of their interactions into transactions, they had more and more to live up to, more and more to account for, and more and more to fight about.

The excessive accumulation of things that people feel they must do is nearly universal in relationships. It was not a particular problem in former times when freedom was only viewed as important and possible for one party, the man, in relationships. You were either a man and in charge or you were a woman in the obedience lane. But today, obligation bloat in relationships is nearly universal, and is universally felt as an infringement on freedom.

> **The excessive accumulation of things that people feel they *must* do is nearly universal in relationships.**

Exercise 2A: Finding Obligations that Are Not Real Obligations in Your Relationship

A clue to determining if an obligation is really an obligation is the presence of a sense of resentment when doing or thinking about an activity. In our example, Tom developed discomfort with "having to" call Sue every day. He felt he was no longer making the call freely. He was no longer doing it just because it would please her, but because she would be irritated if he didn't call. The feeling of discomfort, a sense of being trapped into doing something, is often the reason that people will stop doing the activity, such as Tom not calling Sue for two days. Stopping is fine. But you need to let the other person know what is going on. And you need to know that you aren't in fact obligated to carry out the activity. Otherwise you will be angry and not know why, and end up feeling guilty and not know what you've done, aside from making your partner feel bad.

Practice discovering "obligations" that aren't real obligations by choosing a relationship and looking for three things you do in that relationship that you regularly resent. Here are three examples of non-obligations will help you get started.

Relationship: My marriage.
Example non-obligation 1: My husband, Andy, expects me to cook all the meals and clean up afterwards, while he sits on the couch reading the paper. I certainly feel resentful about this, but have always felt guilty if I blow up and say something. He always ends up making me feel that if I don't cook for him, I don't love him. It's true that when we first went together I really felt good when I cooked for him. But now it's just a chore. I see that we never made a deal that said I had to cook in exchange for him doing something else. I need to talk with him and approach it as finding

ways for each of us to please the other by doing things that we really want to do. We also need to divide up the things that we have to do.

Example non-obligation 2: I always feel as if I have to take the kids to the doctor. It's as if that is my job. We made no agreement about this. It just came about because when they were first born, I was the one who took them. We can talk about this. Maybe it would make sense for me to take the girls and he the boys.

Example non-obligation 3: We always have sex on Saturday night. It makes me feel as if I have no choice. I don't want to keep doing it just because I feel I have to. I think if I told Andy that it is important to me that I feel I have a choice, he would understand. He might feel the same way.

Your Relationship:

_____

Non-obligation 1:

_____
_____
_____
_____
_____

Non-obligation 2:

_____
_____
_____
_____
_____

Non-obligation 3:

_____

_____

_____

_____

_____

By recognizing parts of your relationships that have turned into obligations without ever having agreed to a transaction that made them obligations, you will gradually trim resentments from that relationship. The other side of the coin is to work at building up interactions with your partner. That is, increase the time you spend doing things willingly with no thought of being repaid for them or having your partner respond in any particular way.

Simple conversation counts as interaction if it is not "scripted." That is, if one or the other person isn't editing what they say, keeping in mind that they must not say A, B, and C, and must always say D, E, and F. Freeing up conversation, making it truly interactive, is frequently the best thing a couple can do to improve their relationship. Conversations where one or both parties feel obligated to say what is expected are not interactions.

CAUTION: Abusive, impolite, or offensive language also destroys freely interactive conversation. It turns what is said into an attack.

"Yes, dear," in reply to everything the other person says does not make for interaction, nor is it even conversation. In order to restore conversation that is real, you must become aware of your verbal attacks and criticisms of your partner. You cannot have meaningful conversations with someone you attack and criticize. No one will continue to seek interaction, contribute their thoughts joyfully, and converse at length who needs to modify, edit, and suppress what they think in order to keep from being attacked verbally and sucked into endless heated arguments. "Yes, dear" is much to be preferred. So, if you want to increase communication and conversation with your partner:

- Stop all criticizing, debating, and humiliating.
- Start listening, contributing, and learning.

Often it is a facial expression or body language that chills interaction and immediately turns what's going on into some form of transaction. For example, Tom and Sue are talking about going to the movie.

Tom says, "I heard that the new Disney movie is really good."

Sue looks up from the paper in surprise. "Isn't that an animation for children?"

"Yes, it's an animation, but I heard it's really good and adults like it as much as kids do."

"Who said that?"

"My friend Jack at work was talking about it."

Sue's face looks as if she just drank out of a carton of curdled milk. She spits out, "You mean the guy who's about twelve years old?"

At this point the interaction ceases. From here on Tom will either just shut up or he will attack Sue in return. More than likely the movie planning is over and they will spend an unpleasant evening at home.

Getting as much interaction back into your relationships as you can is worth every effort you give it. Interaction is the "meat and potatoes" of relationships. Freely interacting gives both parties a sense of being at ease, being with someone that they genuinely like, and, above all, a sense of home, of being where they belong.

Exercise 2B: Increasing Interactive Conversation with Your Partner

The goal of this exercise is for you to identify what you say and do that turns conversational interaction with your partner into confrontation or just "please pass the butter" automated exchanges.

Look for three things you characteristically do or say that are likely to be taken by your partner as criticism, disapproval, or outright attack while you are talking together. These examples will help you get started:

Example 1 Typical "Conversation":
Whenever we go out to eat, Henry always asks me where I want to go. I say I don't care. Somehow we always end up fighting.

My Attack or Criticism: I guess I would rather wait for him to suggest someplace and then I can say whether I like it. Often, when he finally suggests a place, I say something like, "We were just there last week." Then he blows up. I guess it wouldn't be much of a chore to just list our choices and say which ones I like and ask him which ones he likes.

Example 2 Typical "Conversation":
When we're watching television, especially the news, Edna will say, "Do we have to watch that?"

My Attack or Criticism: I say something like, "What's wrong with watching the news? You get to watch anything you want before I get home." She often just leaves the room. I guess that's no conversation at all. Perhaps we can talk about what to watch ahead of time. I don't really care that much. I just feel criticized when she shows disapproval of what I have on, and so I criticize her. Why do that?

Typical "Conversation" 1:

_____

_____

My Attack or Criticism:

_____

_____

_____

_____

_____

Typical "Conversation" 2:

_____

_____

My Attack or Criticism:

_____

_____

_____

_____

_____

Typical "Conversation" 3:

_____

_____

_____

My Attack or Criticism:

_____

_____

_____

_____

Partners honoring their transactions—that is, keeping their promises—improves the health of a relationship. Keeping the number of promises made to a minimum also helps. Every relationship needs to have some transactional elements. Marriage has a marriage contract. It usually consists of mutually agreed-on monogamy, sharing of assets, and mutual care of children. Other than these fundamentally important agreements that define marriage itself, few transactions are needed. Perhaps the agreements that roommates might need will suffice for most marriages beyond the marriage contract.

Not having a lot of promises to keep between you and your partner means you are both free to interact without obligation. Without the freedom to give and take without obligation, there can be nothing given freely and nothing received out of gratitude. For love to remain and blossom in a relationship, there must be cracks in the obligations for love to grow through. Love must be freely given. Without the freedom afforded by interactions, love disappears. What will be left are two people dragging themselves through a relationship made up entirely of guilt, anger, and resentment.

Don't imagine that an answer is to erase any and all obligation. That merely ends the relationship. Freedom that matters is made up of choices over and above promises. The basic marriage contract is sacred. It does, however, provide a foundation for the garbage of bloated expectations. It is worth your efforts to clear away the garbage and use the sacred foundation of human trust and mutual agreement for building a love fed with voluntary giving and grateful receiving.

It will be helpful for you to keep a record of your successful removal of unnecessary obligations and fostering of freer interaction in your relationships. You may wish to use your private journal to keep a record of such successes. There is no better learning model than your own successes that you can refer to when you relapse and need help.

Here are two examples for setting up a journal to record your successes. Leave room for six records for each of the two kinds of success:

1. Unnecessary relationship obligations that have been discovered and discarded.
2. Improvements in conversation and other forms of interaction.

Practice Record For Chapter 2

Example 1 Date: 10/4

A Relationship "Obligation" I Discovered and Dropped: My husband keeps after me to lose weight. In thinking about this obligation and free transaction stuff, I noticed to my amazement that I've never made any kind of deal with him that said what I would do about my weight. I think there may have been kind of a deal that said if he didn't get on me too much about my weight then I would ignore his drinking most of the time. But there was no real deal between us and it would be dumb anyway. I feel free for the first time in a long time to deal with my weight however I want. And I'm a lot less irritable with him. He made a reference to it the other day and I just smiled and said, "I feel better taking care of that without your criticism." He's stopped referring to my weight altogether. He seems to be more willing to talk about things that bother him.

Example 2 Date: 10/12

An Improvement in Our Conversations: My girlfriend used to be a lot of fun, and we talked and talked into the night a lot of times. We haven't done that for a long time. After thinking about how criticism stops free interaction and free give-and-take of conversations, I could see how I started sort of taking over our talks. It's as if I thought I was her teacher or something. The other night I asked her what she thought about some people we know. At first she kind of balked and asked me what I thought. I said I didn't really know, and I was kind of confused by them and wondered what she thought. She started to open up and I had to catch myself a couple of times from jumping in and telling her what she ought to believe. After a while it was fantastic. She kept going and told me all kinds of things I didn't know about them. She's a really good observer of people.

Chapter 3
Criticism Keeps Anger Warm and Relationships Cold

"What do you think?" she asks Jerry. Joyce learned long ago never to buy anything for the house without giving Jerry a look at it first. She holds the new drapery material up to a window in the den and looks to see what is on Jerry's face.

She sees his disgust before she hears the words. "That color has a faded look. For heaven's sake, you said you wanted to replace these drapes because they're faded. So you go out and pick ones that look faded when they're new?"

Her jaw set, Joyce begins folding the material away in silence. Jerry notices the start of the silence, as if the electricity had gone off. As his words echo in his head Jerry thinks, "Damn it. Why do I do that?"

Later they eat dinner. It's another formal "Please pass the butter" dinner. They have had hundreds of them.

Jerry's thoughts and feelings alternate every few minutes. He feels a sharp guilt for being such a monster as to attack his loving wife when she is trying to do something for him. He can't bring himself to say he's sorry. He imagines his confession would disturb her angry silence and awaken her full fury.

Then he fights off his guilt with thoughts that justify his critical attack. "She just doesn't have any judgment. Over and over I have to make the choices and do the planning. What the hell would she ever do alone?"

Imagining herself alone is exactly what Joyce is doing. Her fantasy of leaving the marriage has become her refuge during these Cold War tactics. She can go days without "giving in," or treating Jerry pleasantly. It used to last for only a few hours. She used to feel hurt and then want reassurance from him. Now she hardly notices the hurt. She just feels cold and indifferent until her feelings for Jerry stir, usually starting with pity. He starts to look like a lost sheep after a few days.

Criticism is an attack. Critical and judgmental thinking accumulate ammunition for attacks. When we deal with any anger problem, it helps to remember that anger is about control. Habits of criticism and judgmental thinking are like the bark of a herding dog. Constant attention to another person's behavior with critical comments and judgments serves to "head off" behaviors that the critic finds objectionable. Keeping the sheep from straying from the master's chosen trail is the sheepdog's task. Likewise, in the case of relationships: **The purpose of your criticism is to prevent your partner from straying away from doing what you think is the right thing for him or her to do.**

Jerry's anger habit began early in the marriage. He quickly took on the role of "overseer" for the family. It is his job to see that everything that goes on stays on the right track. He is the family sheepdog and the family overseer all wrapped into one. He doesn't necessarily like this role. Most of the time it is painful to him. While the children were growing up and still at home, his critical family role often left him lonely and feeling isolated from the rest of the family. But he thought it was his job to be a shepherd of the family flock for their safety. His view of his wife and children as "sheep" left little room for him to appreciate them as individuals.

Another role of criticism is to keep anger alive and available for exercising control. Anger is a habit. Habits die if they are not practiced. The reason we feel as if other people cause our anger is that the habit is so readily available. Angry thoughts and feelings seem as if they just "pop up" in certain circumstances. It feels as if the people or circumstances that are present "make" the anger "pop up." But it is our habit of being critical that keeps anger warm and ready.

Critical thoughts and judgments keep ammunition for controlling your partner fresh and immediately available.

Anger works like many other habits. If you are in the habit of smiling a lot, then many things will "make" you smile. If you are suspicious a lot, then many things will "make" you suspicious. Anger in relationships follows the same pattern: if you think critically of your partner a lot, your partner will "make" you angry a lot. We will break this problem into two parts so that you can work on stopping it: there is judgmental thinking and openly judging your partner, and there is critical thinking and open criticism of your partner.

Thinking judgmentally or openly judging your partner on a regular basis is one problem.

Judgments create guilt out of facts. For example, if your partner doesn't call (fact), you judge him or her to be guilty of neglect (guilt). Thinking critical thoughts or openly criticizing your partner on a regular basis is a separate problem. Critical thoughts presume that you are in charge of another person's behavior. For example, you fume and squirm while your partner tries unsuccessfully to adjust the VCR.

Let's start with judgmental thinking. Factual judgments are a necessary part of living. "That is a pine tree" is a judgment. "You are my friend" is a judgment. "You are my enemy" is a judgment.

- Factual judgments come down to saying:
"You are X" or "It is an X."
- Judgmental thinking adds another message to factual judgments:
"You are guilty of being an X."

Consider the following statements. Kelly says, "Mike doesn't pick up the towels. He leaves them for me to pick up." You might think that these statements or thoughts can only imply that Mike is guilty of something and therefore they must be rooted in judgmental thinking. But they could be either judgmental or factual, and it makes a big difference which way Kelly meant them.

A judgment of guilt implies that Mike did something he shouldn't have done, and should be punished for it or otherwise be held responsible. A judgment of fact is only a statement of fact.

Example of guilty judgment (Kelly's thought): "Mike doesn't pick up the towels. He leaves them for me to pick up. Just like a man. What a slob." The implication is that being a man means being a slob and men should be ashamed of themselves for being men.

Example of factual judgment (Kelly's thought): "Mike doesn't pick up the towels. He leaves them for me to pick up. I need to tell him I'm not going to pick them up any more."

The key to recognizing guilty judgment is your emotionality. If you can say or think statements with a sense of calm grace, then they are likely to be factual. If thinking and/or saying them starts your "motor running," then they are likely to be judgmental thinking.

Read Kelly's two thoughts in the preceding paragraphs. Notice how one encourages you to raise your voice and the other can be read in a relaxed manner. Judgmental thinking maintains your anger. It makes the distance short between thinking "Mike doesn't pick up his clothes" and verbally attacking Mike when he does anything objectionable or surprising.

You don't have to give up judging.

Avoiding judgmental thinking doesn't mean you can't make factual judgments. Jerry thinks he must stop giving his opinions in order to stop making judgments concerning Joyce. He doesn't need to just blank out. He can turn his judgmental thinking into factual thinking. For example, "Joyce often makes decisions that I don't agree with and think are wrong." This is certainly a fact.

Exercise 3A: Turning Judgmental Thinking about Your Partner into Factual Thinking

---

Identify four judgmental thoughts you often have about your partner. Try to turn them into facts. You may need to revise them. It is difficult to separate judgmental thinking from factual thinking sometimes. Here are two examples to help you:

Example 1 My Judgmental Thoughts:
My husband likes attention from strangers better than he likes my opinions. He just takes off when we are at a party and talks nonsense to anyone who will listen. He never pays attention to me.

Factual Judgment: I guess the facts are that my husband does do a lot of talking to others at social events. He's a salesman and uses these events for making contacts, even though I get left to fend for myself. While he's doing this he's not paying attention to me.

Revision, If Needed: When I read this I still get a little ticked off. Here we go again. My husband is a salesman. He uses parties we go to for finding potential clients. This means that we spend a lot of time apart at these parties. I can read this more calmly now.

Example 2 My Judgmental Thoughts:

My girlfriend thinks she's better than I am. She's always talking about the college she went to and how it's so great, and how her parents make so much money.

Factual Judgment: I guess I don't really know if she thinks that she's better. So, just the facts. My girlfriend does a lot of talking about the college she went to. I never went to college, so I don't really care about that stuff. She also talks about her parents' money sometimes.

Revision, If Needed: I can read these changes with less anger, but I'm still irritated. So here goes again. Sometimes my girlfriend talks about the college she went to. It doesn't interest me much. Sometimes she also talks about her parents' money. She seems to take pride in it. I can read this without getting emotional. It also makes me feel more adult and confident to think like this.

Your Example 1:

_____

_____

_____

_____

Factual Judgment:

_____

_____

_____

_____

_____

_____

Revision, If Needed:

_____

_____

_____

_____

_____

_____

Your Example 2:

_____

_____

_____

_____

_____

_____

Factual Judgment:

_____

_____

_____

_____

_____

Revision, If Needed:

_____

_____

_____

_____

_____

Your Example 3:

_____

_____

_____

_____

Factual Judgment:

_____

_____

_____

_____

_____

Revision, If Needed:

_____

_____

_____

_____

_____

Your Example 4:

_____

_____

_____

_____

Factual Judgment:

_____

_____

_____

_____

_____

Revision, If Needed:

_____

_____

_____

_____

_____

You've probably noticed that as you eliminate judgmental thinking about your partner and make your thinking more factual, a weight begins to drop from your shoulders. This weight is your readiness to attack your partner. Being ready to attack is the very basis of anger, and it is a heavy load to carry around. Dropping it does not involve smothering your anger, it merely means that you don't go around carrying weapons.

Sorting out your critical thinking and judgments gets easier as you begin to have some success. As you distinguish between criticism and factual thinking it will become clearer to you that the criticism is really about anger and control. You will see where criticism takes you and where facts take you. Critical thinking leads to more thoughts of how your partner should change. It leads to what your partner should do. Factual thinking leads to what you can do, namely problem-solving.

For example, "She isn't paying much attention to me lately" leads to thoughts about what I can do to change that. But if the thought is "She's ignoring me just like she always does," then your focus will be on how her behavior is wrong and she should change it.

Critical thoughts and judgments keep anger available. They don't solve anything. Factual thinking helps solve the problem, and it also calms your mind. It promotes the use of reason and keeps you feeling and acting like an adult. Factual thinking helps you solve a problem.

Critical thoughts and judgments keep anger available.

Critical thoughts keep you thinking that your partner is a problem and ought to change.

Factual thinking also helps you have a calm, adult attitude. Once you begin to drop critical judgments and thoughts concerning your partner, you will begin to see how much work they were. In fact, you need to go to quite a bit of trouble to remember your judgments and criticisms. Letting them be forgotten will give you a sense of relief. Your mind will become calmer; it will become easier to smile; and you will become more relaxed. The anger you carry around with you, even when it's low-level anger, is a burden. You can't stay ready to criticize your partner without burning up some energy.

Love does not survive frequent critical judgments from a loved one. The message these judgments send is: "You're not good enough." Over and over—from the way one person parks the car to another's choice of words or likes and dislikes—you aren't good enough. To love means to value another as you value yourself. Ongoing critical judgment sends the message, "Maybe I could love you if you shape up." A partner with reasonably good self-esteem will not settle for such a condition, especially when it is communicated in an unpleasant manner.

The alternative to criticism is talking to each other with respect. The alternative to critical thinking is thoughtful problem solving.

The alternative to judgmental thinking is coming up with ways you can change, not ways your partner can change.

Changing the way you think about the most important person in your life is hard work and takes practice. It will be difficult enough to accomplish without having other people encourage you to keep up critical thoughts. Be careful with whom you talk. What is their attitude toward their partners?

Men and women often gossip in demeaning ways about the opposite sex. The stories and jokes tend to have different themes in women's and men's locker rooms, but both are likely to encourage critical contempt toward a partner. You may find that skipping those after-work trips to the bar or the "nineteenth" hole after golf is a relief to your relationship.

It will help you to make real changes if you keep a record of some successes. Writing down incidents that work out differently and more positively than in the past helps to make actual lasting change. Use your private journal to record five successes in catching yourself in critical thinking and changing it.

The following two examples will show you how to set up your record.

Practice Record For Chapter 3

Example 1 Date: 10/21
Situation and My Thoughts: My boyfriend uses really poor English. I find myself thinking about his bad grammar rather than paying attention to what he's saying. I want to scream at him when he says something like "I seen that movie." I keep thinking, "Why doesn't he hear what he's saying? Is he as dumb as he sounds?"

My Success in Making My Thoughts Factual: These are the facts. I'm embarrassed by my boyfriend's bad grammar. Period, end of story. I asked myself why. I began to see that I view him as if he's an extension of me. After all, it's not me talking. It's him. How he talks is up to him, and how I talk is up to me. Then it occurred to me that there are other parts of our relationship that I've kind of taken over. How he cooks is also his business. How he dresses. A load of worry that's been building up over time started to drop away when I began to see that our relationship is better when each of us is responsible for our own behavior.

Example 2 Date: 11/5

Situation and My Thoughts: I've been used to thinking about my wife as kind of an incompetent airhead for a long time. Yesterday she started to talk about the possibility of moving. I began thinking, "Oh boy, what magazine has she been reading now?" I was about to say something sarcastic to her.

My Success in Making My Thoughts Factual: I caught myself. I said to myself, "Why go down that path? I listen to everyone at work. She's the one I love. Maybe I need to listen and learn to respect what she says." So I really listened to her and asked her questions and she really got going. It turns out that she has a lead on some lake property. She has already checked on it and it is okay for a septic system. The only question is the water supply. We talked all evening about a lot of different possibilities. I began to remember what it used to be like between us.

Chapter 4
Imaginary and Real Relationships

I hear his cheerful salesman's voice at the front desk before I open the door from the waiting room and invite Andy into my office. He gradually stops selling himself as the hour goes on. His voice becomes boyish as he recounts his about-over marriage to Julie. His cheating, lying, and even stealing from her have broken up the marriage. Yet she is willing to give him one more chance if he sees a counselor. Half an hour into his story he becomes plaintive and regretful.

"After all, she's my best friend," he says with a straight face.

I interrupt his story. "That doesn't seem as if it could be true."

Startled, his face reddens as if my comment were a verbal slap that actually reaches his face. He repeats defiantly, "She is my best friend. Why do you say that?"

"Well, you say you lie to her frequently. You cheat on her. You continue to charge to her credit card after you've promised her you won't. My impression of you is that you are easy to like, and we could

> easily become friends. If we became friends, would you lie to me and steal from me? I think what you mean when you say Julie is your best friend is that you like to think of her as your best friend. Perhaps we could say that you imagine her to be your best friend."

Clearly Andy doesn't treat Julie like a best friend, or even a good friend. And if he really wants her to be his best friend—or even a good friend—he will have to do the things friends do. He will never be a best friend to Julie by imagining it is true while continuing to treat her otherwise.

Most relationships have two aspects: one imaginary, the other real.

Marriage is made up of the real marriage and an imaginary marriage. Friendship is made up of a real friendship and an imaginary friendship. Your real relationships are made up of the actual interactions you have—the way you talk with one another, the way you treat each other—and the values you place on one another as demonstrated through placement of trust or distrust, demonstrated gratitude or demonstrated demands. Real relationships are made up of how people behave toward one another.

The real relationship consists of how you actually treat each other plus your actual feelings toward one another. An imaginary relationship is made up of what you tell yourself about how you feel toward the other person and what you tell yourself about how the other person feels toward you. Spouses may have angry feelings day in and day out toward their partners, may treat them as enemies, but still imagine that they love them.

An imaginary relationship consists of a story about how you feel about each other, not the actual feelings themselves. Like any other fiction, imaginary relationships can be more or less realistic.

An imaginary aspect of marriage can represent feelings that are often actually in the real marriage, or it can be made up of ideas about the marriage that rarely or never exist in everyday life. Or it can actually be the opposite of the real marriage. For example, what Andy imagined about his marriage at the beginning of this chapter is quite unrealistic. His behaviors bear no resemblance to "best friend" behaviors toward his wife. In fact we will see that his imaginary view of his relationship to Julie actually helps him cheat, lie, and steal from her.

Many solid marriages are backed by imaginary versions. These serve to get the couple through rough times and make things run smoothly day to day. If a husband approaches his wife intending to tell her a clever story or interesting event and she is busy or in a bad mood and "blows him off," it is helpful for the husband to imagine that she loves him anyway and think of her as tender and caring. Love and care for another is not possible 100 percent of the time. If it were, couples would have no other relationships, no other lives, and no other selves; there would be only their relationship together. "I'm his wife" is the only identity a woman would have if she were totally devoted to her husband. One doesn't always have loving or even caring feelings toward another person, no matter how close that person is. Life is more than one relationship.

A sense of safety and comfort is afforded by a "story" that sustains and affirms one's belief in the other person's love and loyalty in its absence. We learn since childhood to maintain a picture or "faith" in facts, even when the evidence for them disappears. When someone leaves our sight, they still exist, even for a young infant. We go to school out of sight and communication with Mom, but she remains "there," ready to welcome us home. Trouble arises only when our imaginary representation of the absent person bears little resemblance to who they are. Or our view of a relationship not supported by facts blossoms into something terribly unrealistic. So remember: imaginary relationships are valuable to have when they bear some resemblance to the actual relationships, but imaginary relationships are destructive when they vary greatly from actual relationships.

How do you go about evaluating a relationship? How do you tell if the imaginary part of the relationship is helpful or harmful to the relationship? The key to healthy imaginary relationships is whether they lead to expectations that are regularly met, or to expectations that are regularly frustrated. Imaginary relationships are important for getting us through dry spells by imagining that our partners have positive reactions even when they are not feeling or showing those feelings. If the imaginary relationship becomes a way for us to attempt survival in a desert where the feelings imagined are never or very rarely in evidence, then we will eventually die of thirst for those feelings. The imaginary relationship eventually runs out of sustenance, just as a canteen eventually runs out of water.

So, to determine whether your imaginary relationship with someone is helpful or harmful, ask yourself:

- Do I ever actually feel the feelings I think I have toward this person?
- Do I ever actually act on the feelings I think I have toward this person?
- Does my partner ever actually show signs of having the feelings that I imagine her or him to have?
- Does my partner ever actually act on the feelings that I imagine him or her to have?

Exercise 4A: Examine Your Most Important Relationship, Imaginary and Real

Choose your most important relationship. Pick two positive feelings you think of yourself as having toward this person and two positive feelings you think of them as having toward you. How often are these feelings really in evidence by you, by her/him? Here are two examples that will help you get started:

Example 1 Relationship:
My wife is the most important person in my life.
Two Positive Feelings I Think I Have: I think I love her more than anything. I also think I depend on her more than anyone to help me in life.
Evidence of My Feelings: I work hard to buy her what she wants. Maybe I don't tell her, but she should know. I always come home. I don't make a decision without considering how she will take it. Maybe these aren't really evidences to her of my feelings of love and how I depend on her. Actually, I don't really feel love toward her much. Mostly she seems irritated or I feel angry over not having sex. Hmm.
Two Positive Feelings I Think of My Partner as Having Toward Me: I think of her as loving me deeply. I also think she respects me.
Evidence of These Feelings: She never wants sex. But she's always there. She doesn't say much about my job, but she always worries that other people at work are treated better than me and says I deserve to have what they are getting. I guess this is all kind of thin evidence. In fact, she seems to blame me for other people not respecting me as she thinks they should. I don't know if she really does respect me.

Example 2 Relationship:
My boyfriend Jack is most important to me.

Two Positive Feelings I Think I Have: I just love him to death and I want to help him in everything I can.

Evidence of My Feelings: I tell him all the time that I love him. I do little things to surprise him. I try to help him choose better friends to hang out with. He drinks too much and I tell him I don't like it, and I don't have sex with him when he's drunk. He says I don't help him, I just try to control him. Maybe he's right.

Two Positive Feelings I Think of My Partner as Having Toward Me: I know he loves me. He respects me more than any other woman in his life.

Evidence of My Partner's Feelings: We argue a lot and sometimes he gets really angry and leaves. But he always comes back and says he's sorry, and that he loves me more than anything. Even though he sometimes calls me awful names, I know he respects me. Okay, how do I know? Maybe it doesn't show much. His love doesn't, either. Am I just making up the way he feels toward me?

Your Important Relationship:

_____

_____

Two Positive Feelings I Think I Have:

_____

_____

Evidence of My Feelings:

_____

_____

_____

_____

_____

Two Positive Feelings I Think of My Partner as Having Toward Me:

_____

_____

Evidence of These Feelings:

_____

_____

_____

_____

_____

Many couples find that after a while they treat most people in their lives, including strangers, better than they treat each other. Yet they continue to insist that they love each other and are good friends. They imagine that they love each other, yes; but when they examine how they actually act toward one another they see a different story. Learning to create and maintain a good real relationship that doesn't deteriorate into a Cold War kept alive

> **In good relationships people are good to each other.**

by an imaginary view of caring and love isn't rocket science. The opposite of angry, destructive, and uncaring behaviors is loving, helpful, and caring behaviors. In short, in good relationships people are good to each other. Being good to your partner is the way to maintain a good relationship.

The imaginary part of a relationship often hides the real relationship from a couple's perception, even when everyone else can see the reality. The bickering, abuse, depression, and useless complaining are visible to others, but the couple continues to imagine they have a marriage. "Yes, there are problems, but we really love each other and want to make it work." They fail to see they have a bad relationship because they are bad to each other. It isn't their feelings or desires that cause their miserable relationship. It is their behavior. Being bad to your partner is the way to ruin a relationship, regardless of your feelings, intentions, and imagined closeness.

Being good or bad to your partner isn't very different than being good or bad in the moral sense. Most of us would agree that we ought to try to love and protect our neighbors and treat others in the way we wish to be treated. Yet often the very people we proclaim we love are the ones toward whom we do not express love. Places of worship are full of people attempting to learn to treat their neighbors and even strangers as they treat their loved ones. But before we can do that, we need to learn to treat our loved ones lovingly.

Proclamations of love are only intentions to treat someone lovingly, and they are often substituted for loving treatment. Intentions are not virtues and they don't help relationships. They don't count unless they are part of an action. Plans are just plans, they are only as real as the material they are recorded on. Intentions such as those listed below are only an imaginary smokescreen for hiding the lack of a real loving relationship:

- I was going to call.
- I intended to come home.
- I expected to get to it.
- I wanted to be close.

In order build a good real relationship you actually make the promised call; you come home at the promised time; you "get to" the promised task; and you actually become intimate and vulnerable with your partner. To build a good relationship you must stop treating your intentions as virtues for which you ought to be given credit. Just as is the case with the "road to hell," the road to a broken relationship is paved with good intentions. In order to make your real relationship a good one: substitute good actions for good intentions.

Exercise 4B: Substituting Good Actions for Good Intentions

The goal of this exercise is to substitute actions for some of your intentions in an important relationship. Instead of thinking about how you feel, you must act. It is not necessary for you to think about how you love your spouse in order to carry out loving and caring actions. As you learn this basic fact, your actions themselves will start to feel loving. The overall goal is to work toward a good real relationship.

Examine your most important relationship by asking yourself, "What do I intend to do, but do not follow through on?" You will find these unfulfilled intentions in thoughts about what your relationship is like; that is, in your imaginary relationship. These two examples will help you get started:

Example 1 Relationship:
My marriage to my wife Sally.

My Intention: I think I love Sally more than anything. I guess this means that I intend to be kind to her and help her whenever I can, and never hurt her.

What I Can Do to Make Our Relationship Better: I can actually be good to her in the ways that I imagine. I could start by trying always to be kind in the way I talk to her.

Another Thing I Could Do: I hurt her when we go out together and I spend time with other people away from her. I can just stay with her when we are out.

Example 2 Relationship:
My relationship with my boyfriend, Johnny.

My Intention: Well, we always argue when he comes over. When he's not around I imagine us together being good to each other, holding hands, smiling, and talking.

What I Can Do to Make Our Relationship Better: I guess it's true that I intend not to argue with Johnny and not to get mad at him when he comes over. I guess I could really carry through and see what happens. I could smile at him when he comes over, instead of sort of daring him to be nice. I could treat him in a friendly manner no matter what happens for a few times and see the result. If he still acts the same way as he does now, then I'm going to have to think about whether the idea that I have about how he feels about me is just an imaginary thing.

Another Thing I Could Do: Johnny gets hurt and angry if I pay attention to other guys when we are out. I could just stop doing that and treat him like he's the one and only. I guess that's the point of my dreams about our relationship.

Relationship:

_____

My Intention:

_____

_____

_____

What I Can Do to Make Our Relationship Better:

_____

_____

_____

_____

_____

_____

_____

Another Thing I Could Do:

_____

_____

_____

_____

_____

_____

Changing your poor relationships into good relationships takes a lot of practice. Much of this practice is going to be involved with the anger and control problems that arise in many relationships. We will deal with these problems as we go along in the book.

But first, it will be helpful for you to separate your imaginary relationships from the reality of what goes on from day to day. Making a real relationship more like your imaginary version of it— actually loving, actually caring, and actually being mutually helpful—is dependent on your recognition of the difference between what is and what you intend. And, above all, it is necessary to stop thinking that your hoping and imagining your relationship is good is all you are responsible for. Your actions must be good in the most commonsense meaning of the word if your relationship is going to be good. Don't save your "goodness" for strangers when you don't practice it at home.

It will be helpful to keep a record of your progress in your private journal. Set up some pages in the journal, like this example. Leave space in your journal for five records.

Practice Record For Chapter 4

Example 1 Date: 9/3
What I Did to Make Our Real Relationship Better: I used to tease Sam about his hairline. I've been thinking about ways I could really be more loving toward Sam, and it occurred to me that embarrassing someone sure isn't a loving or "good" thing to do. I talked to Sam about this and apologized, then stopped it. It feels good.

Example 2 Date: 9/22
What I Did to Make Our Real Relationship Better: I used to resist when Sally wanted me to help clean the house when we were going to have company. As I started to think more of my real actions toward Sally, it became obvious that she is always worried about how the house looks and it's very unpleasant for her to think of guests seeing dirt and disorganization. I finally saw helping out willingly as a loving thing to do for Sally, regardless of what I think about the house being clean or not. It feels good to do it for her.

Chapter 5
You Are Not Your Partner's Disciplinarian

A black Audi A8 with personalized license plates DLWTHIT forces its way in front of George on the Parkway. George simultaneously applies his brakes, his horn, and his extensive profane vocabulary. For several miles he watches closely for a chance at retribution against the Audi, while his thoughts of torturous revenge on the offending driver also torture him. George cuts off another car as he pulls over for his exit and is home in five minutes.

George's wife hears the door leading from the garage slam and shakes her head and sighs.

"You should have seen it. This SOB in his fancy car nearly killed me. Those people make me so damn angry." George is talking before he is all the way in the kitchen.

"George, don't let it spoil your whole evening. You got home safely. That's all that matters."

> "Stop patronizing me! This guy almost killed me. You and your 'live and let live.' You don't understand what I go through. You never understand. Don't upset me more than I already am."
>
> After fifteen years with George, Susan knows her lines. "You just relax in the den. I'll keep the children quiet so they won't bother you. When would you like dinner?"

As far as George is concerned he's an ordinary guy who is afflicted with lots of things that make him angry. Drivers, his wife, his children, and Republicans all make him angry. Fat cats and stray cats send him into angry dissertations. If you were to ask him why he is angry so much of the time he would blame his wife, his kids, and the awful state of the world.

When George finally agrees to marriage counseling, he recites his list of complaints about his wife to the counselor ending with, "I work my butt off and always have. She sits home and all she has to do is take care of the house and kids. But she just will not leave me alone when I'm home. She always wants something. I'm sick of it. She and the kids are all the same. They have no respect, no appreciation. They just want, want, want. None of them even talk to me unless they want something."

George is sure that his wife makes him angry. Susan has tried to learn how not to make him angry. His children have tried to learn how not to make him angry. Everyone in George's family has tried to take responsibility for George's anger—except George.

Most people subscribe to George's "theory" of anger. As ridiculous as it seems, it is commonly assumed that our partners make us angry. Most people justify their anger by pointing at something someone else does. And, unfortunately, many spouses and children see themselves as responsible for the anger of other family members, just as Susan took it upon herself to try to keep everyone from making George angry. Children learn this perverse theory about anger from their parents and teachers; they learn that they are responsible for other people's anger.

"Don't make your mother angry."

"He pulled your hair because you weren't nice to him. Be nice and you will get along with him."

And worse, children learn that others are responsible for their anger, at least when they can make the proper argument—someone made them angry.

"Why did you hit her?"

"She was making fun of me."

"Jane, were you making fun of him? Don't you know better than that by now?"

The facts are quite different from such lessons about anger that children learn and families practice.

Your readiness to forcefully change something you don't like causes your anger.

The thing you don't like does not cause anger.

When George's wife asks him a question that he doesn't like, it is his habit of attacking her to change her behavior that is responsible for his becoming angry. Susan merely says or does something he doesn't like. When George's children disturb him, it is his habit of using threats that causes his anger. When George blows up at Susan for not properly appreciating his efforts to support the family, it is George's habit of attacking what he doesn't like that is responsible for his anger.

We would all recognize George's responsibility for his anger if he took out a gun and shot his children when they bothered him. It is no defense to say, "They made me do it. They were too noisy." We need to recognize that the anger itself is George's preparation to attack his children. It's his anger and his responsibility.

Relationships are stronger and healthier when both parties "own" their anger. This means that both people readily separate

Relationships are stronger and healthier when both parties "own" their anger.

their discomfort with what their partners do or say from their anger. That allows them to seek other solutions to their unhappiness rather than to become angry and verbally attack each other.

- I don't like what she did. That is a problem for us.
- I'm feeling anger. That is a problem for me.
- I need to get my anger out of the way before I approach solving the problems between us.

Closely associated with the problem of making your partner responsible for your anger is the problem of making your anger responsible for your behavior.

Making *others* responsible for your anger results in an interchange such as this:
"Why did you bark at me?"
"Because you made me angry."

Making *anger* responsible for your behavior results in an interchange like this:
"Why did you bark at me?"
"Because I was angry."

We feel as if our angry feeling makes us act in angry ways. But think about it. Of course angry feelings go with angry actions. But so do envious feelings with cheating and stealing; sexual feelings with sexual acts; and fearful feelings with running away. But envious feelings are not a reason to cheat. Nor are sexual feelings a reason to have sex. Nor is fear a reason to run. Angry feelings are not a *reason* to attack someone. Learning to recognize your angry feelings as feelings is a step toward owning your anger in relationships.

Exercise 5A: Recognizing that Angry Feelings in Your Body Are Different from Angry Thoughts

Recall an incident with your partner when you became very angry. Try to recover the feeling of anger just by thinking about the incident. Work yourself up as best you can by thinking about what happened at the time. Get into the anger. Write a description of what you are thinking in order to "work yourself up."

Then try to pay attention to how your body actually feels. Forget your thoughts for a minute and write down a description of the feelings in your body. Now answer this question: Is there anything about the way my body feels that makes me have to attack? Here is an example to help you:

Incident: My wife got all dressed up before going to work. I was suspicious and followed her at lunchtime. I saw her having lunch and laughing with a man I didn't know. I wanted to kill them both.

My Feeling: My body is tense. I feel an unpleasant strain around my eyes. My shoulders are up a little. As I imagine hitting my wife, I can feel my right hand and arm starting to make a fist.

Is There Anything about the Feeling that Makes You Have to Attack? These are just bodily feelings when I separate them from my thoughts about my wife. But they are not very pleasant feelings.

Incident:

_____

_____

_____

_____

_____

Your Feeling:

_____

_____

_____

_____

_____

Is There Anything about the Feeling that Makes You Have to Attack?

_____

_____

_____

_____

_____

So if your partner doesn't make you angry (in the sense that your partner doesn't make you use angry words or do angry things), your partner is also not responsible for your angry feelings. Your angry feelings are just the sensation indicating that your body is getting ready to physically attack. So what is really the nature of your anger?

Anger is your attempt to solve a problem by seizing control of someone or something. Your anger at your partner shows that you are preparing to control your partner's behavior.

Is there any doubt in your mind that when your partner gets

angry with you, there is something about you or your behavior your partner wants changed? Is there any doubt when your boss gets angry with you, there is something that your boss doesn't like and wants changed? When you do change your behavior because your partner gets mad, don't you often feel resentful at your loss of control, at your loss of freedom? Perhaps your wife always gets angry when you come home late, and so you leave your buddies early in order to get home on time. Don't you feel that your behavior isn't yours, that you are not going home because you want to? Your buddies may have an obscene name for your behavior.

Or you leave your car out in the rain and get wet walking into the house because your husband gets mad when you leave the garage floor all wet. Don't you feel controlled? You feel controlled when you submit to another's anger. So consider that control is what your anger is about, also.

Sometimes you may not even know exactly what your partner wants from you when he or she is angry. But discovering and facing "what is wanted by anger" is a step toward finding other ways for couples to get what they want.

Exercise 5B:
What Does Your Angry Partner Want?

Remember three different times your partner has been angry with you. Write these down, along with what you think he or she wanted. These two examples will help you get the idea:

Example 1: My girlfriend gets really angry with me when I want to watch football on Sunday afternoons. One Sunday she kept after me and then started telling me I'm an idiot and I don't have any taste. She wants to control what I do and what I don't do.

Example 2: My husband yelled at me when I came home with a new dress. He wants to control how I spend my money.

Your Example 1:

_____

_____

_____

_____

_____

_____

Your Example 2:

_____

_____

_____

_____

_____

_____

Your Example 3:

_____

_____

_____

_____

_____

_____

Your partner wants something from you whenever he or she gets angry with you. Anger is an attempt to control. It is easier to see this in others than in yourself. Now try seeing your anger as your attempt to control your partner.

Exercise 5C: What Does Your Anger Want?

Try to remember three times you have been angry with your partner. What did you want? What behavior were you trying to change? These two examples will help you get started:

Example 1: My wife bought this ugly couch. She usually has good taste and I like what she buys. But this time I told her the couch was ugly and she said I could return it if I didn't like it. I blew up at her. I guess I wanted her to be responsible for furniture shopping, but I wanted control of what she bought.

Example 2: I got really angry with my husband when I bought a couch and he said it was ugly. I told him to go change it himself. I guess I wanted to pick out all the furniture, but I wanted to control his agreement with my choice.

Your Example 1:

_____

_____

_____

_____

_____

_____

Your Example 2:

_____

_____

_____

_____

_____

_____

Your Example 3:

_____

_____

_____

_____

_____

_____

At the beginning of this chapter, George and Susan assume that George gets angry a lot at home because Susan and the children make him angry. Once they have made him angry, his anger "makes" him say and do hurtful and destructive things. This view, held by the whole family, including George's mother, makes George the victim of everyone else in the family. In fact, in his view, he is a victim of almost everything that happens in his world. It's difficult to see how such an inversion of what it means to be a victim can get started and remain a part of a relationship for a lifetime—it starts in childhood.

It is easy for children to view their parents' anger as their fault. Anger, unfortunately, is a common part of child management. Parents' anger means to children that they have misbehaved, and their misbehavior is what caused the parents' anger. But adult relationships are between equals. The assumption that one is responsible for the other's anger is an indication that they aren't equal.

One is acting like the parent of the other, or both are acting like parents. As a parent of the other, discipline comes into the relationship. Assuming that you don't believe your partner has the right to discipline you, you have no reason to view your partner's anger as having anything to do with you. And of course the opposite is true. If you do not consider your partner your child, you have no reason to feel that your anger has anything to do with your partner. Your anger is just a mistake you are making about how to bring about change in a relationship between equals. In other words, it is a mistake, and it is your mistake.

George isn't a bad person. George has made the mistake of thinking that others control his anger. A driver cuts in front of him and he is instantly angry, therefore the driver must have caused his anger. The children make noise and he is instantly angry, therefore the children must have caused his anger. Susan doesn't sympathize with him and he is instantly angry, therefore she must have caused his anger. The absurdity of everyone else being in charge of him except himself is lost on George. He and his family don't see how ridiculous it is to believe that everyone in the house except himself controls his angry behavior. He is the angriest member of the household, and he makes the household hell for everyone else.

They fail to see that anger is about control. It is about a habit of controlling by "disciplining" others for things that displease us. Without this knowledge, anger seems like a force. But a force that comes at you from the outside doesn't cause your anger. Your anger comes from inside you. It is a tool you use to try to control others. If there is a lot of anger in your relationship, it is because you and your partner attempt to control each other in order to solve many of your problems.

"Angry discipline" by one person or the other in a relationship causes huge problems. Early in the relationship one or both people may "accept" the right of the other to control them by being angry with them. This produces a relationship where one or both spend time monitoring the other for displeasure. Sometimes this behavior lasts a lifetime.

More often, the role of disciplinarian by another isn't accepted, but the problem isn't dealt with head-on. Instead of simply treating the partner's anger as their partner's problem, they counterattack with attempts to "discipline" the partner for "disciplining" them. Both parties in the relationship have the habit of trying to control with anger what they don't like. Both then carry out their attempts to control each other, and to control the other's attempts at control. The involved arguments that take place between two people who are bent on controlling each other are not a simple matter.

We are all responsible for changing our own behavior. When relationships turn angry it means that at least one person is trying to take charge of the other person's behavior. Anger is a serious and widespread problem in marriage and one-on-one relationships. This is because anger is used by large numbers of people to control others. The use of anger is so commonplace that it is a *habit* for most people. That is why we call it the anger habit.

> **We are all responsible for changing our own behavior.**

Recognizing that you are always trying to establish control with your anger is a huge step for you to take. It will free you from a terrible burden—the burden of running other people's lives. Your relationships will become those between equals if you can locate and give up your attempts to control with anger.

If you haven't yet set up a private journal or diary for recording your successful achievements in overcoming anger, try it now. Set up a practice record for this chapter using the two examples given below as a model. Record your success at recognizing how you get angry in order to "discipline" your partner. Leave space for at least five situations that "made" you angry, but where you were able to see that anger was your attempt to control your partner's behavior.

Practice Record For Chapter 5

Example 1 Date: 8/22
Situation that "Made" Me Angry: My husband came home late without calling. He just waltzed in as if nothing happened and asked how my day was.

What I Wanted: I started to really blow, but the phone rang and he had to spend several minutes talking to someone from work. While he was talking I started thinking, "Okay, I'm angry. What do I want from him? Obviously I want to discipline him about something. What is it? I want him to come home on time or call. But I know that isn't always possible. It's as if I'm ready to punish him to make sure he runs for home whenever possible." I decided I'd better cool my control game and just listen to what's happening for him.

Example 2 Date: 10/2
Situation that "Made" Me Angry: My girlfriend yelled at me for not calling her when I said I would. It really made me angry. She's trying to act like my mother or something.

What I Wanted: After cooling down a while, I realized that I wanted control over how she reacted to me. I wanted to punish her for being upset with me so she would always be friendly to me regardless of what I do. I guess I do need to follow through with what I tell her I'm going to do. I was trying to control her acting like my mother. I guess that means I was trying to "discipline" her for "disciplining" me.

Chapter 6
Self-Induced Unhappiness in Relationships

Shelly hurries to finish the job in the fifteen minutes left until lunch. Ordinarily she would take her time and work through lunch. Shelly never disappoints her supervisor when he needs something.

Her heart jumps as she catches sight of Drew heading for the cafeteria. She smiles as she remembers the musical voice of her favorite aunt coaxing her away from her studies. "That really can wait until later." Each word was higher on the musical scale until the drop in the last syllable beckons her as if she is hearing her name called. Shelly clears her desk quickly, grabs her wallet from her purse, and heads for the cafeteria to meet Drew.

Drew's pained expression is hardly disturbed by his smile as Shelly sits down across from him. Her heart goes out to him. Drew is so unhappy. He stares at a point on the table beside his partially eaten hamburger.

His voice is almost a whine. "I don't know how much longer I can stand it." If someone were to overhear him, they might think he is at death's door with painful cancer throughout his body.

Tears come to Shelly's eyes. "I feel so bad for you. I know you don't want to leave her and lose your children."

"You're such a good person, Shelly. I shouldn't be dumping all this on you."

"I don't mind, Drew. I care for you. I want to share your unhappiness."

"Oh, Shelly. If only I had met you before I got married. You are the only light in my life—except the kids. My wife doesn't care about me. I work and work and she's off with her friends after work. She says I can take care of the kids. I want to be with them, of course, but she spends as much time away from me as she can. And when she's there, she's an unfeeling bitch. When I tell her I'm feeling bad about what's happening, she just shrugs and tells me to do something about it. You're so different from her. I've never felt so much caring and concern in my whole marriage as I have from you in just the last few weeks. And we've never even spent any time really alone."

Shelly's heart pounds as she's thinking, "We really do have a future. He's so lovable. How can his wife treat him like that?"

Drew "suffers through" a divorce made messy and painful by his view that his standard of living shouldn't have to be affected by the change in his situation. Shelly stands by him and sympathizes with all of his complaints. She honestly thinks that his wife is a money-grubber just out to take everything she can get. Shelly gives Drew money to hire another lawyer who is "more sympathetic."

Finally the divorce comes through. Shelly and Drew are married the day after the Final Decree. They start their married life in the house that Shelly had almost owned before she met Drew. She took a large home equity loan out on it to help him fight his wife in court. She now has larger monthly payments than before. Drew has nothing but debt, but they don't care. For now, they are in love.

The foundation for many relationships is the unhappiness of a "Drew." With surprisingly few variations on the theme, Drew will marry twice more in his life. He is an expert at unhappiness and he is also an expert at finding company to share it. He is habitually unhappy. Trying to rescue him from unhappiness is like trying to rescue a fish from drowning in water—water is where fish live.

Unhappiness is the foundation of some relationships.

This is the way it works. A person like Drew (male or female) is very good at demonstrating two things:

1. I have deep and tender feelings.
2. I'm being hurt by an unfeeling, uncaring world.

A person capable of loving and caring is attracted to this combination as they are to an injured kitten. It is not obvious to the caring person that this "kitten" will always appear to be injured, and has nothing really wrong with it except that it gets along by being a victim.

At first it is not evident to Shelly that she will never be able to help Drew feel better. It seems as if she is helping him fight the wicked wife who is so unfeeling toward him and who crushed his tender inner self. Lending solid support, listening to him for hours, losing sleep, lending money—these all serve her desire to help him. They also serve to make her special in his eyes. She is not like his first wife. She is different. She cares. She is sensitive to his inner pain. And like all of us, Shelly is happy being special in someone's eyes.

Even before the divorce is final and they get married, Shelly has some occasional doubts. Her life has changed. She hardly sees her friends any more. Her job is okay, but she doesn't care anymore about doing really outstanding work. Shelly is startled one day when her supervisor stops by her desk and asks if she's okay.

"Why yes, of course. Why do you ask?"

"You just seem different. I thought you might be a little down."

The thought enters Shelly's head once in a while that she has placed helping Drew at the center of her life. She just sort of exists until they are together. But when they are together she loses any nagging doubt she has. It feels so good to be in love with a man who needs her and appreciates her. She has never said no to him.

Within weeks of their marriage, Shelly becomes concerned about Drew in a different way than before. He doesn't seem to be any happier. If anything, he seems more negative about his ex-wife than when they were married and going though a divorce.

After a few weeks Shelly's concern turns to impatience. One day she comes home from work and finds him there already. He usually comes home after she does. She finds him in the living room watching TV.

"I didn't expect to find you home already."

"Oh, I just didn't feel like working this afternoon. So I came home at noon."

"Are you sick? Let me feel your forehead."

Drew's voice rises. "No, I'm not sick. I'm just sick and tired of working in order to pay that bitch child support. She makes more than I do."

Shelly's chest suddenly feels tight. She feels as if she isn't getting enough air. She used to have an anxiety problem, and she recognizes the physical symptoms immediately. She relaxes her shoulders and forces herself to slow her breathing, even though it feels as if she needs more air. She pays attention to the program that Drew is watching and follows it intently with him for a few minutes. By the end of the program she feels more relaxed.

Shelly again turns her attention to what Drew said. What had set her anxiety off? He doesn't want to earn money. They have big debts. She has a big debt. They can just make their payments and his child support as it is. He's frightening her.

"Honey, you have to put your ex-wife behind you. We'll work together and pay the child support. It will only be a few years and that will go away. You're here with me now," Shelly tells him.

"You don't understand—just like she never understood. Are you going to be just like her? Instead of trying to understand me, you start bitching at me. Women are all alike."

Drew leaves the house and heads for a bar.

Shelly sits in the living room crying. "Oh my God," she says, over and over.

Drew comes back later full of apologies, but they have entered a new period in their relationship. Week after week, month after month, there is more fighting. As she loses her appetite for concern for him, Shelly becomes the new "person with no understanding." She takes over as the source of Drew's unhappiness.

After one year of marriage, Shelly calls up Drew's ex-wife. They get together for a talk. They are very much alike, and strike up a friendship. Shelly uses her new friend's lawyer for her divorce from Drew.

Many times the new partner, unlike Shelly, will hang on desperately to their imaginary version of the marriage. When they are "good"—that is, when they baby their partner—things do go pretty well. So they maintain the view of their partners as tender and delicate. In their view it is they who fall short of loving their partners as they should. This can go on for a lifetime.

CAUTION: To be on the safe side, depression should be ruled out before assuming you are dealing with a "Drew."

Inability to experience happiness is a symptom of depression, but it is primarily a disease that affects vitality, one's ability to act. People like Drew are often mistaken for being depressed. They are not. If the person functions well and remains unhappy when they have someone who consistently sympathizes with them, and simply gets angry when they don't, it is not depression. It is a person who uses his or her unhappiness to get support in the form of sympathy and help. The unhappiness eventually becomes real unhappiness. But unhappiness is not depression.

There are degrees of habitual unhappiness such as Drew's. Most of us make ourselves unhappy to some degree for the same reasons as he does. We stay hurt a bit too long. We exaggerate an injury just a little. We hold on to hurt feelings to the point where we must make an effort to remember what the hurt was. The concern of another is precious.

If we are lucky enough to have a caring relationship with someone who calls us on these self-produced miseries, they are short-lived. If your wife says, "Oh come on, you just have a cold. You're not dying," you are a lucky man. If your husband says, "Your friend hurt your feelings and I don't like that. But she's still your friend and I love her for that," you're a lucky woman.

Exercise 6A:
Getting Rid of Habitual Unhappiness

The biggest problem with carrying unhappiness around is that carrying it around really does make us unhappy and angry. Keeping it just to have it to bring out and display when we want sympathy or attention is not worth it. Identifying unhappiness that you can get rid of will improve your quality of life. You will feel better and it will improve your relationships. And, above all, it will reduce your anger.

A handy clue to use in spotting habitual and unnecessary unhappiness is that you usually only feel it when you are talking to someone else. For example, you're having a good day. You meet some friends for lunch, and you find yourself talking about your childhood and how

> **Identifying unhappiness that you can get rid of will improve your quality of life.**

cold your mother was. You feel miserable. Your friends are sympathetic. Was relating your sad story to your friends and receiving their sympathy worth the misery?

Try to find three instances of your "favorite" topics that come out in conversation and make you unhappy. These two examples will help you get started:

Example 1 Self-Induced Unhappiness: When we get together after bowling, the guys sometimes start talking about their ex-wives. I go right along, just as I do at work sometimes, and talk about my first marriage. I end up feeling awful. It's like reliving it all again. I think everyone goes home feeling depressed. It's like a contest to see who was hurt the worst. In the future, when that topic comes up in a group, I think I'll just go home and keep the good feelings I have going.

Example 2 Self-Induced Unhappiness: Sometimes when I'm talking to a couple of my friends I find myself recounting how I've been hurt by someone who used to be a friend. I start to feel the humiliation of the rejection all over again. Maybe I'm trying to tell my friends not to hurt me like that. Maybe I'm trying to recruit them to my side and tell me how bad my ex-friend is. But I see that I don't need to keep going through my hurt feelings like that. It puts a wet blanket on my whole day.

Example 1 Self-Induced Unhappiness:

_____

_____

_____

_____

_____

Example 2 Self-Induced Unhappiness:

_____

_____

_____

_____

_____

Example 3 Self-Induced Unhappiness:

_____

_____

_____

_____

_____

Keeping a laundry list of our unhappy experiences damages relationships in another very serious way. Instances of mistreatment are handy when we fight with one another. But keeping unhappiness around in a relationship is like keeping matches around in a fireworks factory. Past hurts are the meat and potatoes of relationship arguments.

"You hurt me when you danced with Joan at our wedding."

"That's nothing compared to the way you always acted when we were dating."

Keeping a laundry list of past hurtful misdeeds by one's partner is all too common in relationships and especially in marriages. The lists can go back decades. They are the ammunition used in verbal fighting. The "winner" of a relationship argument is the person who has the best record of being hurt by the other person.

Winning a relationship argument is very much like winning a lawsuit. You need a good record of all your opponent's transgressions. The more detailed, the better the chance of winning. You may have experienced being in an argument with your significant other and finding yourself accused of all sorts of dastardly things. You think, or sometimes might say, "I just don't have as good a memory as you for what happened." In other words, you've run out of ammunition.

But keeping all those records around has a big price. They are by nature a history of hurts. Keeping them around is like keeping the stone in your shoe or the thorn in your finger. They keep hurting, become infected, and do systemic damage. On the other hand, throwing these records away means you are no longer prepared to "go to trial." You will be unable to win when you are in a fight with your partner. So you will need to give up the arguing. Throwing away your list of miseries caused by the other person means you're going to have to give up arguing with that person.

Reducing the length of the list of hurts you've suffered reduces your self-induced unhappiness. It also means reducing the role of anger in your relationship. Not a bad deal. But it will still be hard to do. You may feel that you are just "wimping out." You may think that this means letting your partner "get away with anything." Not fighting and not claiming victim status is a viable choice for relationships. It doesn't mean you must be a saint and tolerate everything. It certainly doesn't mean becoming wimpish. It does mean sticking to the original point when you complain. It does mean you give up the role of "judgmental and punishing parent."

For example, if someone regularly leaves their clothes lying all over the bathroom, the typical complaint starts with, "You always leave the bathroom a mess." Two minutes later, it expands to: "You're just like your father. You never give a thought to what I have to do around the house. You never help with anything."

You can learn to keep your complaints limited to the clothes in the bathroom or the laundry that needs doing. If you do, you will soon learn that the anger and even rage you often feel at the beginning of an argument is due to the laundry list of complaints you have in storage, not to the clothes on the bathroom floor. If you throw away the list, you throw away the unhappiness that is always ready to pop out and inflame your emotions, motivate your fights, spoil your day, and worse.

Exercise 6B: Shortening Your Laundry List of Hurts that Make You Unhappy

It's a big step to realize that the hurtful actions of others are still hurting you because you choose to keep them as ammunition. A starting point for reducing these self-induced miseries is to notice the difference between what starts your anger and where your mind and emotions go after that. The clothes on the bathroom floor, this day, this time, are the actual stimulus for a complaint in our example. Beyond that is all "laundry list." The "you always," the "you never help," the "you don't care," and the "you're just like your father," are all things you carry around to hurt the other person with. But they actually hurt you. So let them go.

Try to recall three arguments with someone with whom you have a relationship. Name the original stimulus. Where did the argument go? Name some items on your "laundry list." These two examples will help you get going:

Example 1 Argument:
Well, it was a bit more than an argument. It was a fight that lasted for days over everything you can imagine.

Original Stimulus: I said I didn't like hamburger all the time. So I guess the stimulus was the hamburger on the table.

Where Did the Argument Go: My wife said something like, "Well maybe you should shop and cook the meals." I said something like, "Why do you always have to go off on me? I work my ass off too." She started in on my not helping and I told her she never appreciated a thing I do. This was all a long way from whether we ought to have hamburger.

Items on My Unhappy Laundry List: I guess I often use "you don't appreciate me." And it's true; whenever I do, I really do feel unappreciated and used. Also my wife doesn't always go off on me. When I say she does, I feel like she's a hateful person. It makes me feel lousy when I make out that I'm married to a hateful person. Maybe I ought to just stop using "you don't appreciate me" and "you always go off." I feel better just realizing that this is a problem.

Example 2 Argument:
My husband and I had a fight that lasted all week.

Original Stimulus: My husband sat down to eat dinner and the first thing out of his mouth was "Why do we have to have hamburger all the time?"

Where Did the Argument Go: He irritated me, so I said something like, "Why don't you help with the shopping if you don't like what I buy?" Then he accused me of always attacking him and did his unappreciated poor guy thing. So I said, "What am I supposed to appreciate? You come home and sit on your ass. You let things go in the house. If I didn't nag you, you'd let the house fall down around us." It got worse. Both of us left the table. I went to bed. The hamburger was still on the table in the morning.

Items on My Unhappy Laundry List: I guess I do always accuse him of not doing things around the house. This is actually far from true. I make him out to be some kind of lazy slob, and he isn't. I see now that thinking of him in that way in order to attack him really makes me feel bad too. It makes me feel as if I'm a poor mistreated wife married to an ogre. Yuck. It sounds easier to just stick to the hamburger complaint.

Example 1 Argument:

_____

_____

Original Stimulus:

_____

_____

Where Did the Argument Go:

_____

_____

_____

_____

_____

_____

Items on My Unhappy Laundry List:

_____

_____

_____

_____

_____

_____

Example 2 Argument:

_____

_____

Original Stimulus:

_____

_____

Where Did the Argument Go:

_____

_____

_____

_____

_____

Items on My Unhappy Laundry List:

_____

_____

_____

_____

_____

_____

Example 3 Argument:

_____

_____

Original Stimulus:

_____

_____

Where Did the Argument Go:

_____

_____

_____

_____

_____

_____

Items on My Unhappy Laundry List:

_____

_____

_____

_____

_____

_____

Present conditions in the Western world contain the fewest reasons for being unhappy in all our history. Yet misery is rampant, particularly in relationships. Much of this unhappiness is self-produced and is closely connected to control and anger issues. We often cultivate and preserve our "injuries" carefully for the time when displaying them is useful for either the manipulation of another person's feelings toward us or to outright punish them with guilt for doing something we don't like. In doing so, we not only invite unhappiness into our lives, we preserve and guard its presence like a prized tool for living.

Unhappiness certainly can be useful if controlling and punishing others is our way of life. If we forego anger and punishment and control as our ways of relating to others, we can also give up the unhappiness used in the service of controlling others. If we don't need or want to make others feel bad, we need not carry around our hurts.

Practice Record For Chapter 6

It will be helpful for you to keep a record of successes in removing the sources of your self-made unhappiness. Two kinds of success should be recorded. Watch for times when you have been able to discover and remove your favorite "feel-bad" stories, such as those in Exercise 6A. Also record your success in weeding out laundry lists of injury in important relationships. You may wish to use your private journal to keep a record of successes. Your own successes are the best models for future progress.

Here are two examples for setting up your journal to record successes. Leave room for six records for each of the two kinds of success:

1. Habitual self-induced unhappiness I have dropped.
2. Victim items I no longer store in order to win arguments.

Example 1 Date: 2/13
Self-Induced Unhappiness I Have Dropped: I usually chime in with the women in my church circle about how bad the children are today and what a shame it is that we have to pay such high school taxes with such poor results. I'm through participating in that kind of conversation. It just makes me feel bad, and I'd rather feel hopeful about kids than critical. I feel more together having decided this.

Example 2 Date: 2/21

Items I Have Marked Off My Laundry List of Mistreatments:
I finally realized that every time I argue with my wife, I think of the time she threatened to leave me. I accuse her of not loving me and just using me. This always makes me feel awful. When I decided I could live without carrying that accusation around, I felt like the sun came out. It's just as easy to carry around good memories and make them into hope as it is to carry around bad ones and make them into sorrow. Hope feels a lot better.

Chapter 7
Dealing with Hot Anger

CAUTION: A Note on Physical Violence

Regardless of how your local police, laws, and prosecutor view the matter, angry physical contact by men isn't the same thing as angry physical contact by women.

Angry physical contact or displays by men physically intimidate women. Angry physical contact by women usually doesn't physically intimidate men. Men need to understand that they are quite capable of frightening women. Pushing or shoving a woman up against a wall, or stepping in front of her and not allowing her to leave, is not the same when men do it as when women do. Women may become frightened for their safety and their lives. Men are not usually frightened when women make such moves.

> *Do not physically intimidate or touch your partner in anger under any circumstances.*
>
> Physical attack is, first of all, a criminal matter, and that is the way it should be. When men are willing to attack women, an overwhelming show of legal force against them is the best way to stop them, and perhaps the only way to reduce the chance of their repeating an attack.
>
> For those who can justify to themselves the use of force to get what they want, talk is useless and even counterproductive. They need to know that what they have done is criminal and that force will be used to stop them.

We can deal with making changes in milder forms of angry behavior in relationships in many ways. For example, we can change habits that accompany attempts to control others. We can increase communication and increase interaction in our relationships. But there aren't a lot of ways to cool down anger once we are really upset. The reason "hot anger" is difficult to deal with is that when we're really feeling anger, we find it difficult to think of anything except justifying our anger and how dastardly our partner is for having visited discomfort upon us. Our attention is so narrow that we may as well have thrown away most of our thinking power. We act dumb, we think dumb, and we don't listen to reason.

Many relationships periodically produce episodes of yelling, threatening, and sometimes hitting. These exhibitions occur when one or both people become so angry that they lose their ability to think properly. As anger increases, one's perspective gets narrower. Extreme anger is really a form of tunnel vision. One's thoughts are so centered on injury and attack that reasoning is impaired and actions and words are used that seem crazy when one is calm. When you are angry, you are likely to be destructive because you become less reasonable.

Try telling someone who is angry that they are being unreasonable, that they aren't thinking about this factor or that, or that they are not taking other possibilities into account. It's like talking to a wall. If you think you can become reasonable while you're angry, you will not make a dent in your anger. Reason is impaired while we are angry, so there is no point in attempting to reason yourself out of anger.

We can't listen to reason when we are angry. Think of the times when your spouse was very angry with you and you tried to intervene by being reasonable. Your spouse doesn't listen to reason when he or she is angry and neither do you when you're angry. Your spouse doesn't listen to good advice when he or she is angry and you don't listen to good advice when you're angry. When we are angry and unreasonable and won't follow good advice, we sometimes do some pretty dumb things.

Angry arguments can lead to danger.

People drive dangerously when they are angry. You may be one of them. People attack their spouses and children physically and verbally when they are angry. You are apt to endanger your loved ones when you are angry. And that is because when we are angry, we do dangerous things.

Add it up. When you are angry and fighting with your partner:

1. You are both impaired intellectually.
2. You are both being unreasonable.
3. Both of you are likely to do something that hurts or endangers the other or someone else.

Exercise 7A: Dumb Things You Have Done When You Were Angry with Your Partner

Recall two arguments you have had with your spouse or significant other that resulted in doing something that later seemed dumb. Write down what you did and why it wasn't too bright.

These two examples will help you get the idea:

Example 1 What I Did:

My wife and I got in an argument while we were in the car. I sped up (over the speed limit) on a mountain road. It was stupid because I could easily have lost control and caused a fatal accident. Our children were in the car. It embarrasses me to think about it.

Example 2 What I Did:

My husband embarrassed me when we were out with friends, and I didn't speak to him for two days. It wasn't a very good idea because I was more miserable for the two days than he was.

Your Example 1:

_____

_____

_____

_____

Your Example 2:

_____

_____

_____

Usually marital and relationship arguments start at a relatively low level of emotion. When this isn't the case, when one "comes in hot," the other person needs to stay calm and reasonable. The calm one will keep their wits about them, listen without comment, and when asked for a response, can delay by saying he or she needs to take care of something important. The calm person should not try to intervene in

Realizing that your anger is your problem to deal with is a huge step forward.

the other's anger. Intervention will only escalate the anger and the intervention itself can become a subject for heated argument. "Honey, calm down before you wake the children" is going to be followed by a reply such as, "Since when do you give a damn about the children?"

Remember, when you are dealing with an angry person, you are dealing with someone who has lost a lot of intelligence and perspective. You will not be able to calm him or her down. Only their own efforts and time will calm them down.

Anger is the problem of the person who is angry.

Realizing that your anger is your problem to deal with is a huge step forward. This realization also allows you to stop blaming yourself for your partner's anger. But remember, when trying to intervene in your own anger, you are dealing with someone who is not very mature—yourself.

You can use the facts of anger to your advantage when you try to calm yourself down. You aren't at your best, so why not tell yourself you aren't at your best?

Learn to say:

I'm beginning to feel anger at my partner and I'm not at my best.
   or:
I should keep my mouth shut until I'm calm and can think straight.
   or:
I don't want to react while I'm angry and dumb.

While you are experiencing anger at your partner, your thoughts are dominated by justifications for the way you feel. The only "problem" you are concerned with is showing your partner how awful he or she is, and how he or she is making your life miserable. This "how to make my partner pay" thinking will go on as long as your thoughts continue to stir you up. The only way to end the process is either to go ahead with your attack to the point where you must stop because you have made your partner a victim, or to stop feeding yourself inflammatory messages.

The biggest mistake that people in relationships make is to respond to a sense of being victimized by victimizing the other person in return. An eye for an eye creates two one-eyed people. Both will consider themselves as victims. Both will have ammunition for future attacks. Both will soon lose their other eye. This is the way countries try to "solve" their problems. This is the way uncivilized people like most of our ancestors tried to solve their problems. If you don't stop yourself by waiting for the flame to die, you will "solve" your problems with your partner by attempting to make him or her the victim so that you need not continue to feel like one. The result is that your partner will in turn feel victimized—which he or she is—and will victimize you again.

Border incursions never cease between countries until one stops and talks begin, or until one crushes the other. Problems among racial groups, different ethnicities, and between religious groups follow the same pattern, until a truly civilized person comes along and teaches at least one of the sides not to victimize their victimizer.

The same is true of couples. If you stay with your anger, fan it, and follow its lead, you will go to a place you may not want to go. Anger has only one aim—to attack and subdue the other person. If you let anger dictate what your actions will be, your behavior will not be difficult to predict. Your fate is that of an uncivilized brute who knows only one way to solve problems: attack whoever seems to be responsible.

If you do not wish to turn your life over to anger's pre-set solutions, you will need to learn to reject it, even when it is strong and convincing to you. You must treat anger like a mob of lunatics whose enthusiasm tries to draw you in. You must say to it, "You are not my leader. I will not turn my life over to you to determine." Some of this thinking may sound to you as if you're speaking to a child, but you will not experience these ideas as put-downs. They are complements. They carry the assumption that you can live in a different and better way. You must keep your thoughts about stopping your own anger and waiting for it to pass at a simple level. You will be talking to someone—yourself—who will only be able to follow simple directions. You will not be asking yourself to do anything complicated, only to wait and let your intelligence have a chance to respond when it's not drowned out by your anger.

Exercise 7B: Learning that Waiting Makes It Easier to Resolve Problems

Try to remember two incidents of anger at your partner that were resolved after some time without resorting to blame and verbal attack. Try to remember how—when the anger subsided—other possibilities occurred to you. How did you actually solve the problem?

These two examples will help you see what to do:

Example 1 What I Did:

My wife and I were arguing about whether to buy a crib for our baby, who is due in two months. It was getting rather heated. I thought we could wait until several months after the birth. Beth wanted to get it now. Friends dropped in and interrupted our argument, so I had time to calm down while they were there. Afterward, when I was calm, it occurred to me that someone had told me that expectant mothers want to build a nest. It makes them unhappy when the "nest" isn't complete. It also occurred to me that we had some extra money because we received so many shower gifts. So why not go ahead and buy the crib?

Example 2 What I Did:

I came home from work and Jack was sitting on the couch watching TV. The apartment was a mess. He called out, "What's for dinner?" My anger went through the roof. The telephone rang and it was my best friend calling to tell me she was getting married. We talked for a long time and when I hung up I was calm. It occurred to me that when I come home and Jack hasn't started any dinner or done any chores, I need to stop checking up on him so much. I went into the living room and told him that I don't want to get angry anymore about who is doing what. So I'll order out for myself when I'm tired, and when I feel like it I'll fix him something. Otherwise he's on his own. This started a long conversation, the longest we have had without anger in some time. We ended up by agreeing to try some labor division at home. We wondered if we might even benefit from some counseling.

Your Example 1:

_____
_____
_____
_____
_____
_____
_____
_____

Your Example 2:

_____
_____
_____
_____
_____
_____
_____
_____

Pausing will not help if you continue to think about your partner in an angry way while you are waiting. Like a mob that keeps milling around and inflaming itself with new rumors, angry waiting inflames your anger more and makes matters worse. If waiting is going to help you, you must leave the mob and get far enough away so that you do not hear its shouted slogans. The slogans of anger that keep it alive tend to be littered with statements that are impossible to justify when things calm down. Statements with "always" and "never" are hardly ever true. They seem true when you are angry because they justify anger's pre-chosen solution— "We'll put a forceful stop to this." But even though your anger encourages you to believe that your spouse "never helps you," "is always against you," "will never stand up for you," and "never shows any affection for you," these ideas are not likely to be true. They are anger's slogans, the slogans of the mob that keep you following mob mentality as a solution to your problem. To get away from the anger while waiting for your intelligence to return, stay away from the "always" and "never" statements going through your head:

- He always does this.
- She never cares what I think.
- This always happens.
- He will never learn.
- She's always such a bitch.
- He's always such a jerk.

These are the slogans you must give up if you wish to escape from anger's infectious appeal.

And do not add alcohol. There is nothing like handing out alcohol to inflame an angry mob. Alcohol is likely to inflame your own slogan-driven angry emotions.

Exercise 7C: Identifying the Slogans that Inflame Your Anger

Try to remember two times you have been angry. Try to think of them in enough detail so that you start to feel some of that anger even now. Write down the thoughts that inflamed you. Notice how they are likely to contain "always" and "never." Are these things really true? These two examples will get you started:

Example 1 What I Said:

My wife just will not learn. She *never* pays attention to her driving. She *always* gets to gabbing and *never* looks where she's going. She *never* gives a damn about my concern about her safety. She *always* thinks I'm just worried about the car.

Example 2 What I Said:

My boyfriend *always* criticizes me. He is *never* supportive of anything I do. I *always* support him in whatever he wants to do. He's acting just like he *always* does.

Your Example 1:

_____

_____

_____

_____

_____

_____

_____

Your Example 2:

_____

_____

_____

_____

_____

_____

_____

These are the slogans that keep your anger going and headed toward arguments. They keep you wound up and ready to fight, even when the thoughts aren't expressed. They keep your perspective narrow and focused on what you can attack about your partner. As long as you keep preparing to attack your partner, the anger will stick around and even grow.

Giving up these "slogans" is not a formula for giving in to something your partner has said or done. You are not being advised to just let it pass because it's better to get along. This advice is only about ways to let your anger subside so that you can consider doing something to solve your problem beside attacking your partner and expanding the situation into a fight.

Deciding not to let your anger lead you and your relationship doesn't mean that you give in to your partner. Quite the opposite. You are much more likely to find solutions to what bothers you in a relationship when you are calm, cool, and intelligent. Getting away from angry slogans, getting away from the mob mentality forming inside you, takes practice. Find a counter-slogan that is useful to you even when you are irritated or angry, one that you will listen to. Perhaps one like, "Don't be a jerk!" which works for some people. Just keep in mind that the slogan should be something that will remind you that you are not at your best. Then find ways of helping you when you're angry. How do you walk away from mob mentality, stop the slogans, and wait for some peace of mind before deciding to act or even talk?

Recording successes is the very best way to learn to change your anger. By recording incidents, including small examples, you produce your best learning tool—you as a positive model. Use your private journal to record at least five successes. The following examples will help you set up your journal.

Practice Record For Chapter 7

Example 1 Date: 6/1

Incident: I came home and found that my wife had invited company over for a cookout. I always check with her before having any kind of company. I was really getting worked up when she told me we had ten minutes until they were supposed to arrive.

What I Did: Maybe it was the "ten minutes," but I was actually able to catch myself and say to myself, okay, give this some time. Don't go nuts.

Success: I told myself to calm down and do something else. I got busy with the barbecue and stopped a couple of my attempts to sloganeer. I caught the "I always tell her." As I calmed down, she came outside and said, "Thank you for helping with this. I know we usually let each other know about guests, but I'm trying to recruit this guy, and he's leaving town in the morning. Thanks for being you." I really felt good about the whole thing.

Example 2 Date: 6/14

Incident: We were getting ready to go on vacation and my husband kept telling everyone to hurry up as if we were late for a plane or something. It really irritated me.

What I Did: Fortunately before letting him have it, I remembered to calm down and get my perspective back. I stopped thinking, "He always spoils things" and started thinking instead about packing the car and making sure the children had everything they needed.

Success: When we finally got in the car, for once everyone was calm and happy. I said, "Honey, we're going to have a good time. You've earned this vacation, so let's relax and have a good time." He smiled and said, "I guess it's going to take a while for me to unwind."

Chapter 8
Replacing Self-Importance with Gratitude

Fred eases his three hundred pounds into his favorite chair in front of the TV. He notices too late that the remote is on the TV out of reach. His deep smoker's voice resounds throughout the house. With water running in the kitchen sink, Fred's wife Alice doesn't hear his yell at first. As she turns off the water, her humming of her favorite song from *Beauty and the Beast* is also turned off by Fred's bellow.

Alice hears her name being yelled about every ten minutes when Fred is home. It was easier taking care of small children, she thinks. At least they didn't want something every ten minutes.

Alice used to love to wait on Fred. Then, when Fred Jr. was born, it became too much. It was like being a single mother with two children, except one of them was bigger than her and very spoiled. She wonders what happened. How did she get into this situation?

She tries and tries to please Fred. She often wakes up at three in the morning with dark thoughts. Mostly she thinks about Fred Jr. He seems to be turning into his father. She tries not to think of that as a bad thing. Alice tries to remind herself of how proud she is that Junior is going to college. But at three in the morning her fears take her elsewhere. Ugly pictures of Junior's demanding ways, his "forgetting" to return things he borrows, and his nasty temper when he isn't given what he asks for force their way into her mind like unwanted aggressive guests. Alice worries about Junior.

As she enters the living room she sees Fred's angry face.

"Why do you always put the remote on the TV? I don't sit on the TV. I sit over here. You never do what I ask."

Her mind spins. "*Never* do what you ask?"

A blinding flash goes off in Alice's head. At first she thinks she's had a stroke. Then she suddenly feels lighter than she has in twenty years. She can almost fly. Suddenly Fred's anger doesn't matter. Alice turns and heads for the bedroom, tossing her kitchen apron aside as she walks. She packs some clothes and leaves the house.

What happened here? Clearly Alice finally freed herself from the task of feeding a bottomless pit. There is nothing wrong with Alice. She knows that she needs to give in order to be happy. She loved Fred and tried her best to make him happy and look out for him. She didn't make him happy, but she tried.

What about Fred? How did an ordinary guy who was loved by a good woman turn into such a petty tyrant? The answer is difficult for most of us to understand and identify with because most of us suffer to some degree from Fred's problem. Fred feels he deserves everything he wants from those who love him. Why? Because he thinks that because others look out for him he is an important person. Fred believes that his importance to those who love him entitles him to everything he wants from them.

Most of us are self-important to some degree.

Self-importance is the natural side effect of the nature of love. Love is given as a gift or not at all. This means that love cannot be given as a reward or as a payment for something we do or don't do. It is simply given, deserved or not.

We don't realize that we receive love without it being owed to us.

A loving relationship requires the ability to be grateful for what is given for free. For love to be given, it must be received. Like a letter, if love is sent and not received, it is lost. There is hardly anything more frustrating than to try to give a gift to someone who cannot say "thank you" and instead attacks you or asks for even more.

For example: "What would you like for dinner?"

"I'd like steak. Do you suppose you could cook it the way I like it for once?"

Yet, most of us don't fully appreciate what others do for us without our having to pay for or arrange anything. Our conversations from which we learn and are entertained, the words that lift our spirits, the demonstrations of care and concern, and probably most important, the "little" things like the smile on a grandchild's face are given to us for free. We can never earn such things as these.

Because friends and family do so many things for us "for free," but not for others, it is easy for us to think that we have some special quality that makes us deserve all these gifts. We are fed without having to cook food. We are clothed and kept warm without having to pay for it. We are pampered and made a fuss over without having to know or do anything to "deserve" such attention. So we must deserve these things. That is, we think we are loved because we are important to others. Often we don't understand that we are loved unconditionally. We believe we deserve what we actually get for free.

People are obligated to give deference to and follow the instructions of important persons.

Judges, teachers, parents, political figures, and police are obeyed and given respect and deference because they are important people. The mistake we make is to think that anyone given deference and whose demands are met must be important. If you are president of the United States, then others respond to your needs because your office demands deference. It is a logical fallacy to conclude that if others respond to your needs, then you have a right to demand deference. Others care for us out of love and concern, not because we have a right to their love. Love is given to us as a gift.

> **Others care for us out of love and concern, not because we have a right to their love.**

Our response to the caring of others should be appreciation, not self-importance.

When we are given love and care by others, our self-importance leads us to believe we deserve what we get, and probably deserve more than was given. Our parents give us everything we have for many years, and we often think that they should have done even better for us. The world gives us beauty, air, water, and much more that we didn't "deserve" and didn't arrange and didn't pay for. Instead of learning to say "thank you," we learn to demand even more than we receive. It is easier for us to learn to demand more than we receive than to learn gratitude for what is given out of love and caring.

Fred was unlucky enough to marry a good woman. His self-importance bloomed and grew like a cancer with her love and sacrifice feeding its growth. He is not a bad man. He is badly mistaken about why his wife and others answer his demands and attend to his needs.

Alice is finally freed from the treadmill of her one-way relationship with Fred by the realization that it is impossible to continue loving someone who is incapable of gratitude. She finally understands with horror the implication of Fred's words, "You never do what I ask." He isn't aware that doing what he wants is always what she has tried to do. Alice finally realizes that Fred is not aware that she loves him. She realizes that Fred will never be aware of her love. He will always think she owes him what she does for him. Alice realizes in a flash that the very thing she has always wanted to do in a relationship—to love another person—is impossible to do with Fred. He will never accept her love. She is utterly alone.

Exercise 8A: Identifying My Self-Importance in My Major Relationships

A good clue for hunting down your self-importance is the use of the words "should" and "ought to" when thinking about what your loved ones and friends do for you. These words amount to a declaration of entitlement. It is likely that phases such as the judgments "you should do A or should have done B" get their judgmental force from the sense that someone owes you and isn't paying. You feel entitled to make demands of them. That's fine if they really do owe you something. But most of the time others don't owe us anything.

Try to find three self-important claims of entitlement that you make in your important relationships. These two examples will help get you started:

Example 1 Relationship: Mother
My Self-Important Demand: My mother drives me nuts with her calls all the time. I certainly feel that she should stop calling and bothering me as much as she does. She keeps asking me how

things are going. I hardly ever have anything new to tell her or that I want to tell her. Looking at my strong feeling that "she shouldn't" do this, I can see that I really have no basis to judge what she "shouldn't do." Yes, it bothers me, but…oh, I see now. It bothers me so I think she "should" do something about it. Wow. It's kind of a doublethink. Because she loves me I have the right to demand that she take care of my discomforts. But she is one of them! So she ought to leave me alone. Suddenly I have a different feeling about her. When I think of all the things I've expected her to do just because I needed them done or wanted them done, it makes me think I've been a baby for a long time—too long.

Example 2 Relationship: Marriage
My Self-Important Demand: My wife never listens to me. I tell her to be careful with the car, and she has an accident. I tell her not to give in to the kids all the time, and she spoils them rotten. I have a strong feeling that she should listen to me and do what I say more often. So why do I have such a strong feeling that she should…I guess she doesn't owe me that any more than any other woman I know owes it to me to listen to what I tell them. Maybe I do feel that "if she loved me" she would do as I say. She would take care of my needs. This is strange and new to me. I've always taken that for granted. I suddenly have an image of us moving more independently, but having stronger feelings toward each other.

Relationship:

_____

_____

My Self-Important Demand 1:

_____

_____

_____

_____

_____

_____

_____

Relationship:

_____

_____

My Self-Important Demand 2:

_____

_____

_____

_____

_____

_____

_____

Relationship:

_____

_____

My Self-Important Demand 3:

_____

_____

_____

_____

_____

_____

_____

The cultivation and practice of gratitude will make you much less angry and much less demanding with the important people in your life. The confusing part for some is that they feel they have more self-esteem when they act as if they are entitled to special treatment. When a stranger—a clerk in a store, an airline employee, or just a stranger on the street—ignores or treats them as if they are unimportant, they feel compelled to prove otherwise. At home, if they feel they are ignored, they demand attention, sometimes blaming family inattention for their low self-esteem. This behavior is just part of an anger problem and has nothing to do with self-esteem.

Self-importance is very different from self-esteem.

Self-esteem is nearly the opposite of self-importance. Self-esteem consists of an attitude you have about you. It says, "I don't know how I will cope with this problem, but I believe that I will cope with it and do it well, even really well." Having high self-esteem, feeling confident that you can face the future, even if you don't know all you'll need to cope with, doesn't necessarily mean you will not also have a self-important attitude. But it is easier to let go of your self-importance if you have high self-esteem. You don't have to face the fear that you have nothing to fall back on if others don't give you what you demand.

- Self-importance makes demands on others.
- Self-esteem furnishes confidence that you can face your own problems.

These are not truly opposites, because you can have both self-esteem and still feel self-important. It is easier to recognize your self-importance if you have self-esteem. You immediately see that you have a lot to gain by being genuinely grateful for what is given to you. Yes, you can handle your problems, but the love of others is like a refuge that lets you relax and enjoy your life.

A common problem that makes gratitude difficult for many people is the assumption that if you give credit to others, you lose credit yourself. This is as far from the truth as one can get. You lose nothing and gain everything by cultivating gratitude. The opposite of thinking that you deserve what you get (self-importance) is the knowledge that another person loves you.

Your reward for cultivating your capacity for gratitude is the conviction that others love you.

At the beginning of the chapter, Fred has no idea that Alice loves him. His self-esteem is so low that it will be very difficult for him to ever realize this love. He is unable to be grateful to Alice, so he is unable to acknowledge her love. In order to feel gratitude, he risks giving up the attitude that he is responsible for every good thing—and Alice is responsible for every bad thing—that happens to him. This would confirm his worst fears: that he makes mistakes, doesn't know everything, and isn't important at all. Your "reward" for hanging onto your self-importance is the constant fear that it is an illusion. Like the emperor in the children's story, you may end up finding that you have been naked all along.

Exercise 8B:
Cultivating Gratitude in My Relationships

Choose two of your most important relationships, at least one being a member of your family of origin—mother, father, sister, or brother. Describe at least three gifts you receive or have received from each one that you don't ordinarily think of as gifts.

There may be a tendency to think of the things you did or do for that person and try to "balance the scales." Try not to do that. This is about things that are done with no expectation of payback. The goal is to help you see that the demands you make of another person because of your self-importance have no validity. Others give to you out of their love. These two examples will help you get started:

Example 1 Relationship: Father
Overlooked Gift 1: I guess I never thought about it before that Dad gave me the gift of being my father. He could have just ignored me and gone on his way. He spent a good portion of his life worrying about me, trying to teach me, and working for the things he gave me. That's pretty general, but sure worth saying thanks for. I remember once he took me to the zoo and I got tired and he carried me around on his shoulders all afternoon.

Example 2 Relationship: Husband
Overlooked Gift 1: I do demand a lot from my husband. He gets irritated after I ask him to do several things. I can see that I don't show, or even experience, gratitude when he puts up curtain

rods or goes to the store to get something I need. More often I feel that he hasn't done it quickly enough or well enough. Yet he keeps trying to help me. When I start to think of being more grateful for these things I have a different feeling about us, a warmer feeling. Maybe he does love me.

Relationship (family):

_____

_____

Overlooked Gift 1:

_____

_____

_____

_____

_____

Overlooked Gift 2:

_____

_____

_____

_____

_____

Overlooked Gift 3:

_____

_____

_____

_____

_____

Relationship:

_____

_____

Overlooked Gift 1:

_____

_____

_____

_____

_____

Overlooked Gift 2:

_____

_____

_____

_____

_____

Overlooked Gift 3:

_____

_____

_____

_____

_____

Discovering your self-importance and cultivating gratitude in its place is not something you can just do once, like having your gall bladder removed. Self-importance is like a weed in the garden; it keeps sneaking in and you need to keep weeding it out. Every time we encounter praise, have a success, get a promotion, or are deferred to in any way by others, we are in danger of "puffing up." This does not mean that we must learn to practice false humility and undervalue anything we do. It does mean that we take pride in what we do, not in ourselves for doing such things. It means getting outside of our self-absorbed concerns and focusing on what we are doing. For example, athletes need to concentrate on the game, not on their playing of the game. If the game is won, pride can be taken in the win and their teammates, not in themselves for producing it. Writers need to concentrate on the quality of the book, not on their writing of the book. If the book is successful, pride in that success can be

Self-importance feeds the desire for power and notoriety.

taken, like pride in a child who is doing well. Perhaps our most important challenge is to concentrate on the health and welfare of our loved ones, not on our having helped them. Play for the sake of the game; write for the sake of the book; love for the sake of the loved one.

Self-importance feeds the desire for power and notoriety. Gratitude feeds the desire to serve. For self-important people, public office or high position in any organization means power and prestige. For those who experience gratitude, these things mean an opportunity to help others and possible satisfaction in doing so.

Because self-importance arises from our relationships, it will harm our relationships to some extent. Self-importance is a stage built exclusively for the performance of angry, demanding scenes with others. Once built, the stage will be in use.

Often marriages are made up of two self-important people. They both constantly question the love of the other because the other does not tend to their demands. The result is continuous war over whether they are loved. "You don't love me," becomes a battle cry.

For the sake of your relationships, and also for the sake of a more satisfying and peaceful life, it is worth learning to watch yourself for signs of self-importance and for lack of gratitude. It will help you establish the habit of monitoring your self-importance and gratitude if you keep a log of your successes in your private journal. Here are two examples of how you might set up your journal entries:

Practice Record For Chapter 8

Self-Importance
Example 1 Date: 10/21
Self-Importance I Weeded Out: At dinner last night we were all laughing and joking when Sammy, our fifteen-year-old son, made a joke about my bald spot and needing sunglasses at the table. The kids all laughed and my wife joined in. I kind of froze. For a second I felt I was going to say something critical to Sammy. The phrase "self-important" popped into my mind and I started laughing. It really was funny and it felt good not to have to "make" Sammy treat me with some kind of phony respect. He would do anything for me.

Gratitude
Example 1 Date: 10/27
New Feeling of Gratitude: I've been working late a lot and haven't had much time at home. I was beginning to feel uneasy about not having time for the children. Just after I got home tonight my wife rolled in with the kids in the car. She had just picked them up from practice and lessons. I started to think, "Oh great, dinner isn't ready." For once, a bell went off in my head. I started thinking that she was filling in for me with the kids, as well as doing all the stuff she usually does. I went over and put my arms around her and the kids and said "thank you." We had a heck of a lot better evening than I was headed for.

Chapter 9

Substituting Respect and Individuality for Anger and Secrecy

Tina, her wrinkled forehead fast defeating the purpose of her weekend facial, unleashes her sporty little Z4 Roadster to well above the speed limit. Both hands welded to the wheel, she maneuvers through the afternoon traffic in her monthly race to beat her husband home. As she turns into the home stretch, her knuckles turn white as her breath automatically expels in a hoarse "Oh no!" She can see Bill walking up the drive toward the house, head bowed, looking through the mail cradled in his giant bricklayer's hands. As she drives in, Bill continues, head down, through the front door. He is still studying the credit card bill that Tina raced home to intercept. She has successfully hidden its existence from him for over a year.

As Tina climbs out of her car her forehead smoothes. By the time she reaches the front door she has on her game face, the fixed blank expression with fiery eyes that opponents saw when her team was behind in high school basketball. She's ready for the battle.

"After all the financial hell we've been through, how could you do this again? And you do it again behind my back. How do you think we're going to ever pay this off?" Bill waves the envelope.

Tina doesn't flinch during Bill's outburst. When he pauses she says in an even, firm voice, "The card is mine. I ran it up. I'll pay it off."

Her simple statement seems to inflame Bill more than ever. He moves quickly and unpredictably around the room, as if unable to contain an eruption of energy. Tina has never seen Bill lose control and has never been physically afraid of him. His sudden movements startle her. She takes a different tack.

"I'm sorry, Bill, but I just have to have extra money sometimes to run the house. We have so many bills. And customers expect me to be well dressed. What we earn doesn't always stretch. Things are picking up at work and I should get bigger commissions. I'll pay the card off. Don't worry about it."

While Tina tries to explain why she ran up nearly fifteen thousand dollars in debt and also tries to reassure her husband that he will not have to worry about paying the money back, Bill stares at her with a face that looks as if he had just stepped in dog manure. His disgust settles over Tina and drives her away into a lonely and frightening place, like a terminal diagnosis from a cold and impatient doctor. Shame flows into that space behind her eyes. She wants to hide. The time her mother caught her with grown-up makeup on her face flashes through her mind. She feels humiliation such as she hasn't felt since childhood.

Tina has just suffered a blow to the very center of her life as an adult—her adult self has been injured. Who we are, our very selves, consist mainly of our relationships. Tina struggles to keep her relationship to her husband an adult relationship. It has just now changed into something else. She's not a child, but she feels less than an adult in relation to her husband. How did this happen?

First, it is important to realize that this crisis is not mainly about the money involved. Neither Bill's angry reaction nor Tina's credit card use were driven *principally* by concern over money. One of the biggest problem areas in relationships, especially in marriages, is the issue of independence. For Bill and Tina, independence means different things. For Bill, it means going off the reservation. Tina is confused about what it means. Neither of them understands that two people do not become one in a relationship without one of them losing who they are.

It is a common practice to include a ritual of unity in marriage ceremonies. Each person takes a small lighted candle, from which together they light a larger "unity" candle. Often they then blow out the individual candles. Symbolically they have enacted a major danger for their marriage, not the ideal state of the marriage. What this ceremony represents is a loss of individualities. Two people cannot maintain a relationship when they become one person, just as two companies cannot maintain a relationship when they merge into one. One thing, one organism, requires one management. Marriage, if it is seen as a transformation of two into one, requires that at least one of the two lose their individuality. Lighting a symbolic candle as part of a marriage ceremony is a healthy start to a marriage if the couple understands that their marriage is a third thing (a new family), not the only thing (their merged selves). A marriage consists of three things: two people and a family.

In Tina and Bill's marriage, there are three distinct identities:

1. Tina
2. Bill
3. Tina and Bill as a family

Tina and Bill are not clear that they don't need to sacrifice themselves as individuals in order to make a marriage. Yes, they will often sacrifice something of their own in order to help the other person—their time, their energy, or their belongings. But this does not require sacrificing any part of their individualities. Each person as an individual must decide these sacrifices, not some melded entity. Much less should it be decided by one of the two acting as the manager for the marriage.

From the beginning Bill believed that being married—or even going together—meant that Tina should not do anything that displeased him. For him, the heart of her love was for her to share everything and do nothing on her own. Doing something that he didn't approve of without his knowledge meant that she didn't love him and only stayed married to him in order to use him for some personal reason. Bill believes that being married means that if Tina acts without his approval or knowledge, she is violating their marriage, their love. Therefore Bill experiences Tina's independent action as rejection of his love.

Good relationships, and marriages in particular, require both persons to maintain their individuality.

Unfortunately, Tina tried to adopt the "we are united as one" version of the marriage. She has been uncomfortable with that idea from the start. First, it is clear that Bill is more interested in monitoring and passing judgment on Tina's behavior than she is on noting his behavior. When he wants to buy a new exotic "toy" for his workshop, she doesn't object and even shares his joy. When she wants to replace an appliance, or buy a new outfit, or even join a book club, Bill is full of skeptical questions about whether she really needs to do these things. "Why do you want to buy books? You can always go to the library for free."

Bill takes the position that if she loves him, Tina ought to take his discomfort with her activities to heart and not make him unhappy by doing things when he objects to them. Consequently many of their arguments concern her "requests" and his "unfairness." Their version of "united as one" is:

- When Bill wants to do something, Tina usually asks that it make him happy.
- When Tina wants to do something, Bill usually asks that Tina not make him unhappy by doing what she wants to do.

A second problem for Tina with the "united as one" view of their marriage is her gnawing discomfort that somehow she has gone backward in her life when she married Bill. She has this feeling because she did indeed take a step backward, not toward childhood, but toward being less of a person. Every time she "gives in" to the loss of her self-determination in order to keep her husband from feeling she doesn't love him, she becomes less of a person and more of a tool of someone else.

Any loss of wholeness as an individual is universally accompanied by discomfort.

The reason Tina experiences feelings of a child being "caught" by her mother when her husband "catches" her using a credit card is that she experiences the loss of being a real person as she did with her mother. That loss is responsible for her feeling of humiliation in both cases.

Now we can see more clearly why Tina, a savvy businessperson, does such a dumb thing as to run up a lot of debt at 20 percent interest. She knows better. She knows about the power of compound interest. Yet she spends secretly by charging stupidly. Every time she thinks about what she's doing she feels bad. Yet every time she does it, it feels good. It feels as if she is doing something on her own again. She feels free. Secret spending is Tina's bid to keep her independence while maintaining the appearance of obedience.

Good relationships, and marriages in particular, require both persons to maintain their individuality. It is a mistake to think that two individuals can't make it together. Being individuals is the *only* way to make a marriage that is comfortable, loving, and respectful for both persons.

Exercise 9A:
Ending Your Sneak Attempts at Individuality

Many arguments and the resulting alienation in marriages and close relationships result from "offenses" that look and feel like children sneaking off to a forbidden swimming hole. That is, they are often astoundingly dumb or dangerous actions that are meant to be kept secret from a partner. They occur because people feel freer and more like adults when they determine their own behaviors. These behaviors are healthy in one sense: they represent attempts to maintain individuality. However, they are unhealthy for the relationship and sometimes have bad financial or health results.

A valuable approach to improving a relationship is to identify these "sneak attempts" at individuality, and replace them with a more realistic view of the relationship, a view where two people cooperate without giving up their self-determination as individuals.

Try to describe two ways you attempt to maintain your independence in a relationship. Find two ways your partner probably tries to achieve the same thing. These actions are likely to provoke guilt even though you or your partner may defend them when you are discovered. Once you find these ploys ask yourself, "Would I or my partner ever do these things if we felt as independent as we were before we were in this relationship?" These two examples will help you to get started:

Example of My Attempt at Individuality: I often stay out with my friends much later than the time I tell my wife I'll be home. She's always mad and we argue. Sometimes we call each other names. Things are miserable for a day or two afterward, sometimes longer.

Would I Do This if I Felt as Independent as I Did Before the Relationship: It's kind of stupid because I feel miserable the next day and don't get much done. I stopped staying out late like that years ago, when I was single. I guess that's really why I do it; it makes me feel single again. Not that I want to be single, I just want to feel as I did then. As if I'm in charge of my life. Maybe we don't respect each other's independence.

Example 1 My Attempt at Individuality:

_____

_____

_____

Would I Do This if I Felt as Independent as I Did Before the Relationship:

_____

_____

_____

_____

Example 2 My Attempt at Individuality:

_____

_____

_____

Would I Do This if I Felt as Independent as I Did Before the Relationship:

_____

_____

_____

_____

_____

_____

Example of My Partner's Attempt at Individuality: I've asked my wife not to shop at an expensive department store near us. Or at least to compare their prices elsewhere. She continues to shop at the store year after year.

Would My Partner Do This if He or She Felt as Independent as Before the Relationship: This is interesting. My wife always complains about how expensive things are and how she doesn't have enough money. When I first knew her she was really thrifty and took care of herself well and was happy doing it. She's smarter than I am about most things. Maybe continuing to shop at the most expensive store gives her the feeling that she's independent again.

Example 1 My Partner's Attempt at Individuality:

_____

_____

_____

_____

Would My Partner Do This if He or She Felt as Independent as Before the Relationship:

_____

_____

_____

_____

_____

_____

Example 2 My Partner's Attempt at Individuality:

_____

_____

_____

Would My Partner Do This if He or She Felt as Independent as Before the Relationship:

_____

_____

_____

_____

_____

The assumption that one needs to lose autonomy or independence in a relationship in order to maintain love and intimacy is like saying you have to become part of something to love and care for it. In order to maintain a healthy relationship, two people need to remain two people. Complete unity with the other person would be like being married to yourself. In any case, there is a part of us that fights the loss of individuality tooth and nail. We react to the loss of autonomy in such arrangements by staking out secret areas of noncooperation where we can feel the fresh air of individual self-determination.

Another contributor to the formation of secret areas is the development of aversive practices with each other. Trying to control other people's behavior by punishing them when they don't comply with your wishes may lead to surface agreements. But when they are out of your sight they are apt to do as they please, or even do the opposite of your wishes just to assert their right to control themselves.

Verbal attacks, judgments, or any other "punishing" attempts to change your partner's behaviors are likely to drive the behaviors out of your sight. Punishment works very well to change behavior. It's just that the change you get is hardly ever the change you were after.

Tina and Bill, like most couples, have a long history of attacking each other with disapproval, disgust, and outright verbal attacks. The uncomfortable feelings they have when they are under attack from the other are made up, in part, of humiliation that they are not competent enough to run their own lives. Each attack says to the other person: "You are incompetent and you need a parent to run your life."

Attacks threaten to make the other person feel as if they are in grade school and the teacher grabs the chalk out of their hands and says, "You can't do that. The answer is this!"

Attacks always contain a threat of humiliation.

When you hear someone say, "My husband or wife is never wrong," it means that there are heavy threats of humiliation being tossed around in the relationship. No one gives in easily if it means being humiliated. Jokes about men never asking for directions arise from attacks in relationships that translate "doing it my way" into "your way is laughable and ridiculous."

Where you find these complaints, you are sure to find "secret areas" of self-determination maintained by one or both parties that are safe from attack by the other person. The answer to unpleasantness caused by attempts to punish one another in order to change one another is:

- Each person in the relationship is still a person and has the right to determine his or her own behavior.
- Cultivating respect for the other person as a free individual avoids attacks and threats of humiliation.

Exercise 9B: Building Respect for One Another

Building respect toward another does not mean building approval of the other person's behavior. Respect for your partner is like respect for the flowers in your garden. You wouldn't think of trying to spray paint your yellow tulips to make them red. They are what they are. Your partner does things that you like and don't like. You can communicate without attacking in an attempt to "spray paint" them. Your partner is a human being. Human beings change their colors on their own. Talk to your partner about what bothers you. Don't try to change your partner. If you try, you will end up battling, keeping secrets, and feeling alone.

The best source of good information that will help you build respect for your partner is his or her good friends. These are the people who are least likely to be trying to change a person. Moving toward their view of your partner will be a step in the direction of respect.

Identify three characteristics that your partner's friends see in him or her. These are likely to be things you saw in your partner when you first met and have since forgotten. Make a plan to cultivate each of these views.

CAUTION: If drinking buddies are the only friends your partner has, your partner most likely also has a drinking problem. If so, it must be dealt with before anything else is likely to be worth the effort.

These two examples will help get you started:

Example 1 Characteristics My Partner's Friends See:
Charlie's friends all say he would give anyone the shirt off his back. He will go anywhere, anytime, to help one of them.

My Plan: This is pretty hard to think about. I'm used to being angry with Charlie when he spends time helping a friend instead of being at home. But I'll try. Yes, it's true that I saw him as being very generous when I first knew him, and that was part of his attraction. Maybe I can see this as part of him again without feeling it's something I should change to keep him home. Maybe I could go along with him sometimes or drop over to see him later. I'll try.

Example 2 Characteristics My Partner's Friends See:
Sally's friends often depend on her for advice. They think of her as being wise and helpful to others.

My Plan: I do remember thinking this about her too when we were first going out. She seemed like an understanding and accepting person. She didn't preach, but tried to make me feel better. I've lost sight entirely of that about her. I guess it's because of our fighting. I'm kind of excited about bringing back that feeling about her.

Example 1 Characteristics My Partner's Friends See:

_____

_____

My Plan:

_____

_____

_____

_____

_____

Example 2 Characteristics My Partner's Friends See:

_____

_____

My Plan:

_____

_____

_____

_____

_____

Example 3 Characteristics My Partner's Friends See:

_____

_____

My Plan:

_____

_____

_____

_____

_____

Substituting respect for attempts to control and replacing secrecy with a sense of self-determination are worthwhile goals to work on in any relationship that has gone the way of Tina and Bill's marriage. Tina has mistakenly tried to give up her hard-won sense of being an adult who has the freedom of self-determination. She thought that getting married meant she should somehow turn her self-determination into a muddled merger of mutual decision-making. Her attempt is being countered by a part of her that would rather make even stupid moves than lose her self-determination.

Certainly partnerships require mutual consent in order for individuals to do certain things. Even roommates require mutual consent for certain things. But it is necessary to have two actually self-determined people in order to have mutual consent. Two separate people can make an agreement to do whatever they can agree on. Two people trying to act like one person can't make any kind of agreement that is voluntary. The resulting "agreement" isn't an agreement at all. It is the will of one or the other or of neither.

For two people to agree there must be two people.
For two people to love one another there must be two people.
For two people to comfort each other there must be two people.

Keep yourself and your partner both alive.

Bill and Tina lost their original appreciation of each other, and with that, their respect for one another. They no longer live as two self-determining individuals. They live as two people in a relationship that is made up of wounding each other and wearing each other down.

Change takes practice. As with other lessons, it is helpful for you to keep track of successes as you attempt to restore respect and individuality to your relationships. Use your private journal to record these successes. The examples below will give you an idea of how to set up your journal. Leave room for at least six records of success.

Practice Record For Chapter 9

Example 1 Date: 12/22
Gain in Individuality and Respect: Juan used to treat me with what I thought was respect. After a while I realized that his version of respect was a kind of woman-worship and just the opposite of respect. Yesterday I finally told him to cut the crap and treat me like a person, not just a woman. He finally seemed to understand that I don't want him to put me on a pedestal. I want him to listen to me the way he would a good friend.

Example 2 Date: 1/4
Gain in Individuality and Respect: Terry came home in a miserable mood. My first impulse was to tell him I'd had a bad day too and to can it. I caught myself and suddenly a picture of the two of us feeling sorry for ourselves sitting in a cartoon frame came to mind. I guess it woke me up to who we are. Terry is a caring guy who has bad days when he doesn't feel he's very effective with clients. He was that way when I met him and he's still that way, thank God.

Chapter 10
Restoring Communication in Relationships

Celia and Al say their good-byes to the party host at eleven. Smiling and joking, they make their way out the front door, waving cheerfully from the car at Al's boss, Charlie, standing on his front walk.

As Al backs out of the drive Celia asks, "Are you okay to drive?"

"You're never concerned about *me* so you must be afraid I'm going to wreck your new car."

"I'm just asking if you have had too much to drink and drive. For crying out loud, I can't say anything to you without you blowing up."

"Right. I notice you had a lot to say to Charlie. You two must have been over there in that corner for an hour."

"For heaven's sake. You're complaining about Charlie and me when I'm there trying to butter up your boring, insipid, drunken boss. And you're out there enjoying yourself, dancing with that girl who's probably Ruthie's age. I can smell her perfume from here."

> "Who asked you to do any buttering up? You did enough buttering up with that guy you used to work for."
>
> Celia and Al continue the argument into the night. By two in the morning neither can remember how the argument started. By then Celia is raking Al over the coals for the way he behaved the night before their wedding twenty-two years ago. Al is well into his established routine that nothing he has ever done in twenty-two years has satisfied Celia.
>
> When Celia and Al attend their first marriage counseling session, the first words spoken are, "We just can't communicate."

Celia and Al are not alone. Lack of communication is the most frequent complaint that counselors hear from couples. Why?

The goal of communication is to exchange information. The goal of anger is to control another person's behavior. Words can be used for both communication and anger, but they can't be used for both in the same relationship. This is because we do not always tell the truth when we are seeking to control with anger, and telling the truth is essential for communication.

You will not believe your spouse if he or she, while arguing, says you have never done anything to help anyone in your life. But what about the next day when your partner says that he or she didn't mean what was said? Then you have to decide what to believe and what not to believe, what's being said for its effect on you (control) and what's being said sincerely. After all, if your spouse can say "I hate you" without it being true, maybe he or she can say "I love you" without it being true.

Communication suffers if anger is part of the relationship. Management and labor, once they become angry, do not trust what is said. They view what is said by the other as attempted manipulation. Former friends, once they start fighting, no longer believe each other. Parties involved in lawsuits would often make even more extreme claims about each other if their lawyers didn't filter out the more unbelievable renditions of reality.

Divorce is a lawsuit and is often the final showcase for a couple demonstrating the triumph of anger over communication. Once communications are injured by anger, reestablishing communication in a relationship is difficult, but quite possible. It makes all the difference for two people when they are able to talk to one another and be heard and believed. A good place to start is to understand how relationship arguments are typically structured. The hidden goal of relationship arguments is to establish that you are being more badly treated than your partner.

> **Communication suffers if anger is part of the relationship.**

Relationship arguments are about who is the bigger victim.

Angry arguments are like anger in general—they are about control. Even though the words and thoughts are about money or children or in-laws or attention or sex—or even about communication—arguments are about getting control by establishing that you are distressed. You are not only distressed, but are suffering distress because of your partner. Not only that, your distress is far worse than anything you've caused for your partner, ever!

Celia and Al, who introduce this chapter with an argument, spend their evening demonstrating that regardless of how much pain the other person claims to have suffered, the other has suffered more. Al feels irritation when Celia asks him if he is fit to drive. He counters with the charge that she cares more about her car than she cares about him. She continues that he "always" blows up at her. He counters that she's fooling around with his boss. She replies that he's fooling around with someone young enough to be his daughter. By the end of the night they are each claiming life-long hurts and injuries that the other one has inflicted.

Their interchange demonstrates the core problem caused by the anger habit in relationships. The original problem, whether or not Al is fit to drive home, is never addressed. Instead, Al experiences Celia's question as an attempt to hurt him. He runs with the hurt and accuses her of giving him pain. She runs with his response as an attempt to hurt her, and so on. At no time is the original problem addressed. Instead of problems getting solved, an escalating control struggle takes place. Solving problems requires that we think and talk calmly, while trying to be accurate and truthful in our description of the problem. Control struggles require drama in place of real description, rhetoric in place of truth telling, exaggeration in place of factual reports, and feigned or self-induced suffering in place of reassurance.

Relationship anger is due to automatically trying to solve problems by seeking control over the other person by attacking that person. Automatically using control to solve problems guarantees that arguments will revolve around gaining the high ground (making oneself out to be the real victim). The original problem becomes a starting point from which many past charges and counter-charges arise again, therefore the problem doesn't get solved. Truth is sacrificed in favor of drama.

Let's imagine that Celia and Al were actually trying to communicate. First, is there anything they say in their original exchange that they could keep? Out of everything that's said during the whole evening, the only factual statement appears to be Celia's protest, "I'm just asking if you have had too much to drink and drive."

This statement was not believed to be factual by Al. He took it to be a lie. He believed that Celia was trying to control him. The argument had already started and truth was already a non-issue.

The argument started with Al's statement, "You're never concerned about me...." He started what otherwise might have been a sensible conversation about who should drive home, making an exaggerated claim of hurt.

Changing your habit of arguing into a habit of communicating requires that you refrain from using these kinds of "argument starters":

- You're always after me.
- You don't care about me.
- I can never trust you.
- You never cooperate.
- You never help me.
- You never understand.
- You always embarrass me.
- You never support what I want to do.
- You never listen.

Don't imagine that you can start a conversation and actually communicate with statements such as these. Argument starters have two things in common:

1. They are not truthful.
2. They claim that the other person has hurt you.

The words "never" and "always" render argument starters untrue. It would take a really dedicated person to always or never do something. The truth is likely to be, "Last night you didn't listen" or "Sometimes you don't listen."

Exercise 10A: Replacing Argument Starters with Communication Starters

Think of five arguments with your partner. Identify the argument starter. Change the argument starter into a communication starter. Then change what you have written into something factual.

These two examples will get you started:

Example 1 Argument Starter:
My husband called and said his daughter phoned him at work saying she wanted to stay at our house next weekend. This isn't her regular weekend with us. My husband told her it would be all right. I said, "You never consult with me. You always just go ahead and make the arrangements you want to make."

Make the Argument Starter into a Communication Starter:
Well, I guess after I calmed down I could have said that we needed to talk about how we are doing with visitations by each of our children. Maybe I could tell him that it frightens me when plans are made without me. I have a lot of baggage from my first marriage and sometimes I need my husband to reassure me that he isn't going to take over like a Nazi or something.

Example 2 Argument Starter:
My girlfriend asked me to go with her to the doctor to discuss how we might use some other form of contraception. I said, "What's wrong with the pill? You're always trying to change things around just for the hell of it and I'm the one that pays the price." She got all upset and said I never give a damn about her health as long as I can "get some." That really hurt. We didn't have sex for a week.

Make the Argument Starter into a Communication Starter:
I guess I didn't really understand why she wanted to go to the doctor. Apparently she's read some stuff that has her worried about staying on the pill. I could have simply asked her if she was concerned about something.

Your Example 1 Argument Starter:

_____

_____

_____

_____

_____

_____

_____

Make the Argument Starter into a Communication Starter:

_____

_____

_____

_____

_____

_____

_____

Your Example 2 Argument Starter:

_____

_____

_____

_____

_____

Make the Argument Starter into a Communication Starter:

_____

_____

_____

_____

_____

_____

_____

Your Example 3 Argument Starter:

_____

_____

_____

_____

_____

_____

_____

Make the Argument Starter into a Communication Starter:

_____

_____

_____

_____

_____

_____

_____

Your Example 4 Argument Starter:

_____

_____

_____

_____

_____

_____

_____

_____

Make the Argument Starter into a Communication Starter:

_____

_____

_____

_____

_____

_____

_____

_____

Your Example 5 Argument Starter:

_____

_____

_____

_____

_____

_____

_____

_____

_____

Make the Argument Starter into a Communication Starter:

_____

_____

_____

_____

_____

_____

_____

_____

Relationships cannot tolerate mistrust and remain satisfying. Because anger and conflict generate exaggerations and downright untruths, they undermine communication and reduce trust. In order to be open, we risk that our partner might find something in what we say that could be used against us in a fight. If I say I'm troubled lately by doubts over my competence, I risk my partner twisting this later into an attack. For example, my partner might call me a loser who can't be trusted to maintain a job because it's beyond my competence.

Anger drives out communication by driving out trust.

The phrase "good faith" describes what must underlie communication in relationships. What you say may be correct or incorrect, but it must be said in good faith. And your partner must believe that what you are saying is said in "good faith."

If you develop a reputation with your spouse for shaving the truth, and then you are wrong about something, your spouse will assume that you knew the truth and lied. For example, your spouse wants to go fishing and you say that you think it's going to rain. If it doesn't rain, your spouse will assume you just predicted rain to try to prevent the trip. Yet if you and your partner have established "good faith," you need not be right all the time. There isn't going to be a trial if you are wrong about something.

Good communication tolerates error.

If you have established an adversarial relationship, errors are weapons to be snatched up and used. Like a hawk looking for a naive young rabbit, spouses watch for mistakes to use as food for argument. Adversarial relationships make errors costly to the relationship. If you find that being wrong feeds the anger between you and your spouse, you have an adversarial relationship. Communication isn't going to occur until you can both make mistakes without hiding them and without fear of them being used against you.

It has been said that fighting is healthy for relationships and that what is required is to learn to express anger constructively. This amounts to following some basic rules while arguing. The problem with this approach is that that while we are angry we are also not very intelligent. Following rules that require judgments—such as don't lie, don't exaggerate, and don't humiliate—is not likely to ever happen when people are angry. These rules really amount to saying, "Don't argue."

It will be helpful if you understand that your anger has a goal and a method—to solve a problem with your partner using punishment. It will also be helpful to see some alternatives or approach problems in a more friendly way.

Exercise 10B: Understanding Why You Fight and How You Can Avoid Fighting

---

In order to stop fighting you need to know what you fight about. We know, without even looking at your arguments, that because your partner is angry, you wanted something and tried to control your partner in order to get it. Communication requires a friendly approach to your partner. If you want to make something happen with your partner, friendliness is the only alternative to anger and force.

Start changing fights into communication by remembering three fights you've had. Determine what you wanted, then write down what would have been a friendly approach to what you wanted. These two examples will help you get the idea:

Example 1 The Argument:
My wife and I argue about the kids a lot. I think she treats her children differently than mine. I asked her why Sam Jr. couldn't go to Cedar Point on his birthday, a trip we made with Judy, her ten-year-old. My wife blew up and said I never back her on anything, and Junior just comes whining to me to get his way. She said she had told Junior when we went to Cedar Point on Judy's birthday that we'd go again on his if he got his grades up. We fought about whether that was fair and about Junior's schoolwork.

What I Was Trying to Accomplish: Junior and my wife obviously don't get along. I was trying to get her to treat him better so that he doesn't feel as if she hates him.

What Is a Friendlier Approach: I see what this exercise is getting at now. I've got a public relations problem on my hands. I'm never going to solve it by making my wife feel guilty or by attacking her. I need to find some ways to get Junior and my wife together. Maybe I'll wait until I hear her say something positive about Junior and then tell him about it. And I can tell her how much it means to me that she said it.

Example 2 The Argument:
My husband never talks to me. Once again I asked him to turn

off the TV and just sit and talk. He turned off the TV and just looked at me and finally said, "So what did you want to talk about?"

I got angry as usual and said, "Just forget it."

He looked disgusted and said, "What's the matter with you?"

Then we were off and running. We argued all evening. I finally went to bed, but I couldn't get to sleep. He sat downstairs with the TV on.

What I Was Trying to Accomplish: I was trying to get my husband to talk to me. I feel as if we live in the same house, but that's about it. I feel so lonely and isolated sometimes. He will pretty much do what I ask him to do, kind of like a robot. But that's not what I want. I guess I want him to talk to me because he wants to, not because I ask him to. So I guess it doesn't make sense for me to try to make him talk to me. I'd have to write a script for him to read and that would be silly.

What Is a Friendlier Approach: I don't see how I can ever make my husband want to do something. I can probably get him to spend more time, but how could I make him want to talk with me? Maybe the word "friendly" is the key. Maybe I could concentrate on being friendlier. In the meantime, I can do something about my loneliness. I can call a couple of friends I haven't seen for a long time. Maybe I can arrange some outings and ask my husband to come along. He'd probably like a baseball game. I'm beginning to see that I could get back to the person I was when we first met. My happiness wasn't dependent on him then. We did things together because we wanted to and had fun. Maybe I can start acting like that again. Maybe he'll come along. It will be up to him.

Your Example 1 The Argument:

_____

_____

_____

_____

_____

_____

What I Was Trying to Accomplish:

_____

_____

_____

_____

_____

_____

What Is a Friendlier Approach:

_____

_____

_____

_____

_____

_____

_____

_____

_____

Your Example 2 The Argument:

_____

_____

_____

_____

_____

_____

What I Was Trying to Accomplish:

_____

_____

_____

_____

_____

_____

What Is a Friendlier Approach:

_____

_____

_____

_____

_____

_____

_____

_____

_____

Your Example 3 The Argument:

_____

_____

_____

_____

_____

_____

What I Was Trying to Accomplish:

_____

_____

_____

_____

_____

_____

What Is a Friendlier Approach:

_____

_____

_____

_____

_____

_____

_____

_____

_____

Communication of the sort that enriches a relationship must be voluntary for both parties. Each person must feel _free_ to tell the truth, _free_ to reveal faults, _free_ to talk about dreams, and, above all, _free_ to become vulnerable to a partner. Anger, argument, and adversarial bickering reduce these freedoms. Who wants a relationship that requires protecting oneself from the other party? Sharing a dream could be used to humiliate you in an argument. Sharing a secret sensitivity could be used to torture you when your partner is angry with you.

Angry relationships produce secrets. When people aren't sure of what can be used against them, they guard information. There is always a defense attorney in their heads advising, "Don't say anything." With secrets comes the death of meaningful relationships. Trust is replaced by suspicion. Idle chitchat is replaced by silence. The feelings of attraction and love are replaced by memories of attraction and love.

Turning back from arguments and reestablishing communication in your relationships is hard. You are so used to justifying everything you say to your partner and feeling hurt by what your partner says that it is difficult to drop the fighting stance and cultivate a friendly approach.

Angry relationships produce secrets.

Perhaps you are lonely enough or tired enough that the prospect of making friends again has a strong appeal. In any case, it will require practice. The patterns you and your partner are in are habits, and it takes a lot of practice to overcome habits, especially where anger is involved. But isn't a good life with your partner worth the effort?

Make room in your private notebook for keeping track of successes like these two examples. It really helps to write them down. It helps you remember what to do. It gives you a sense of progress.

Practice Record for Chapter 10

Example 1 Date: 4/22

Success: My boyfriend never says he loves me. I complain about it frequently, and we just get into an argument. It occurred to me that what I really want is reassurance about his feelings for me. I had the bright idea of asking him one night how he thought people expressed their feelings toward one another. He started slowly, but after a while he became quite animated about his belief that words don't mean much and the importance of actions and reliability and just being there. Then he got into his childhood and we talked in a way we haven't ever talked before. I think I'm going to be a lot more pleased when he calls regularly and does nice things for me in the future.

Example 2 Date: 4/25

Success: My wife asked me to go to church with her and the kids. It irritates me when she asks me and I started to say something like, "If you want to waste your time with those hypocrites…" But I caught myself. It dawned on me that we don't do that much together. One of us is always going someplace, and the other takes care of the children. Church is a perfect place where we can all go together and then maybe do something afterward. I told my wife what I was thinking and she beamed. I love it when she does that. We talked all day.

Index

H

Humiliation, Threat of 114

I

Independence vs. Dependence
    107–110, 113
Individuality 105–110
Intentions vs. Actions 42–43
Interaction 9, 11
Interactive Conversation 17

M

Marriage/Relationship 2, 36
    imaginary 37–38, 41, 45
    real 37

O

Obligations, Not Real 13, 15, 19
Obligations, Real 13
Owning Your Anger 50, 81–83

P

Physical Violence 77–78

R

Respect 105, 118–119

S

Self-Importance 91, 93–95,
    102–104
Self-importance vs. Self-esteem
    98–100

T

Transaction 9, 11, 19
Trust, Lack of 130–131

U

Unhappiness, Self-Induced
    61–72

V

Voluntary Association 4

About the Author

Carl Semmelroth, PhD, has been in full-time private practice as a psychologist for over thirty years. He received his doctorate in psychology from the University of Michigan in 1969. After spending a year as a National Research Council Associate in Washington, D.C., he joined the psychology faculty at Cleveland State University. He received tenure in 1972 and remained Associate Professor of Psychology at CSU until 1975.

Dr. Semmelroth and his wife, Sara Semmelroth, MSW, ACSW, then moved to Michigan and formed a private mental health practice. Over the years he has also taught graduate classes in theories of psychotherapy, developmental psychology, and lifelong development for the University of Michigan and Western Michigan University.

Dr. Semmelroth has worked extensively with clients experiencing depression, anxiety, panic, and marital and post-traumatic problems. He has also worked extensively with young people hospitalized with serious psychoses.

His journal publications have been in the areas of perception, language development, mental health worker supervision, university teaching, and classroom management.

For more information, go to www.TheAngerHabit.com.